South Korea

South Korea

BY BARBARA A. SOMERVILL

Enchantment of the World™
Second Series

CHILDREN'S PRESS®

An Imprint of Scholastic Inc.

New York   Toronto   London   Auckland   Sydney
Mexico City   New Delhi   Hong Kong
Danbury, Connecticut

Frontispiece: **Seoraksan National Park**

Consultant: Roald H. Maliangkay, Head, Department of Korean Studies, Australian National University, Canberra, Australia
Please note: All statistics are as up-to-date as possible at the time of publication.

Book production by The Design Lab

Library of Congress Cataloging-in-Publication Data
Somervill, Barbara A.
  South Korea / by Barbara A. Somervill.
      pages cm. — (Enchantment of the world)
  Includes bibliographical references and index.
  Audience: Grades 4–6.
  ISBN 978-0-531-21255-4 (library binding)
1. Korea (South)—Juvenile literature. I. Title.
  DS907.4.S66 2015
  951.95—dc23   2014031112

1 2 3 4 5 6 7 8 9 10 R 24 23 22 21 20 19 18 17 16 15

Military band, Deoksugung Palace, Seoul

Contents

Left to right: **Mount Daedun, Jeju Island, students, Mount Hambaek, farmer**

CHAPTER 1

An Unexpected Haven

United States president Bill Clinton once called the Demilitarized Zone (DMZ) in Korea the scariest place on earth. The Demilitarized Zone that stands between South Korea and North Korea, on the Korean Peninsula in East Asia, is the most heavily patrolled, heavily fortified border between two nations.

Over the centuries, Korea has often been under the domination of other nations. In the aftermath of World War II, when the Japanese were forced from the peninsula, two governments were established in Korea. The Democratic People's Republic of Korea, in the north, was communist, meaning that the government owns the businesses and controls the economy. The Republic of Korea, in the south, was opposed to communism. Both sides believed they should be the government of all of Korea. From 1950 to 1953, North Korea and South Korea, as they are commonly known, and their allies fought a bloody war for control of the Korean Peninsula.

Opposite: **A South Korean soldier stands guard at the DMZ. Soldiers have patrolled the DMZ continuously since the 1950s.**

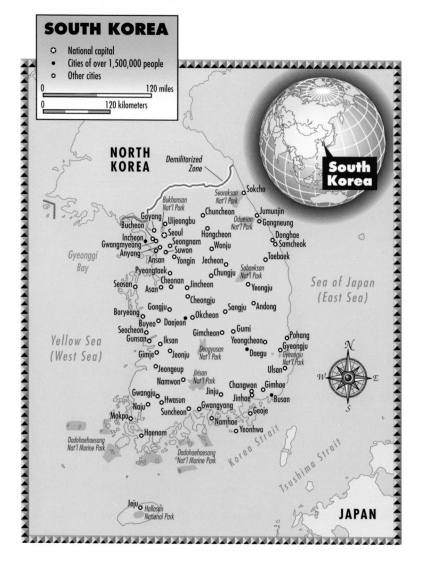

When the Korean War ended with neither side gaining the upper hand, the DMZ was created as a border roughly along the 38th parallel, or line of latitude. The DMZ measures about 2.5 miles (4 kilometers) wide and 150 miles (240 km) long, forming the northern border of South Korea. A high chain-link fence topped with barbed wire and spirals of razor wire are intended to protect South Korea from a North Korean invasion. The DMZ runs up and down mountains, over rivers, and across wetlands.

Although it is heavily militarized, this buffer zone between North and South Korea has become an unexpected haven. Ordinary citizens are forbidden from entering the DMZ, which makes it ideal for wildlife. Amid the land mines buried in the ground and various North Korean tunnels, plants and animals have found a safe home.

The area is a preserve for eighty-two endangered animal species, including the goral, a relative of the goat. Scientists allowed into the zone for research have recorded 2,900 plant species, seventy mammal species, and 320 types of birds. Many believe there are more species yet to be observed. There is even hope that the Korean tiger and the Amur leopard may still live in the DMZ, although none have ever been spotted there.

The Korean War devastated the Korean Peninsula. Cities were flattened, and more than two million people died.

White-naped cranes search for food near the border between North and South Korea. Several hundred spend the winter in the DMZ each year.

The region is a rest area for migrating birds, including several rare and endangered cranes. White-naped, red-crowned, and hooded cranes rely on DMZ wetlands both as resting sites and winter homes. Ruddy kingfishers and Von Schrenck's bitterns visit the flatlands in the summertime. Tristram's white-bellied woodpeckers, now extremely rare, provide a rat-a-tat-tat in the mostly silent DMZ forests.

In the years since the end of the Korean War, North Korea has become a brutal dictatorship and South Korea has become a democracy. Neither side trusts the other, but there is sometimes a small glimmer of hope for a better relationship. In recent years, some South Koreans have been allowed to enter North Korea to visit relatives they have not seen in decades. But this easing of ill will between the two nations is fragile. There have been disputes and skirmishes, but so far they have not erupted into a larger conflict.

Hopefully, peace will come eventually, and the DMZ will cease to exist. What, then, would happen to the many rare species that inhabit the region? Jeong Hoi-seong, president of South Korea's Institute for the Environment and Civilization, hopes that the DMZ would become a wildlife reserve. Jeong says, "The South needs to find a way to incorporate economic benefits with environmental cooperation," to preserve the wildlife of the DMZ. A permanent wildlife refuge would serve as a symbol of peace and a bridge linking the two parts of the Korean Peninsula.

In 2014, some siblings were reunited for the first time since the Korean War. They had been separated for more than sixty years by the border between North and South Korea.

CHAPTER 2

The Stepping-Stone to Asia

ROUGHLY TWO BILLION YEARS AGO, KOREA WAS A land bridge connecting Japan to the rest of Asia. The land's foundation was a mix of granite and limestone, and the land itself was sloped west, toward the Yellow Sea. Over the eons, volcanoes bubbled and spewed lava, and mountains rose in the eastern part of Korea. The peninsula became a land of jagged mountain peaks along the east coast and flatlands and marshes in the west.

Volcanoes continued to erupt, producing a splattering of islands along the western and southern shores. Eventually, the sea covered the land bridge. Korea was now a separate peninsula with hundreds of outlying islands.

The Peninsula

North Korea and South Korea occupy the Korean Peninsula. The Demilitarized Zone marks South Korea's northern border

Opposite: **The rocky peaks of Mount Daedun rise above the thick forest in western South Korea.**

with North Korea. On all other sides, South Korea is surrounded by water. To the west lies the Yellow Sea. To the east is the Sea of Japan, which in Korea is known as the East Sea. And along the south, the Korea Strait separates South Korea from Japan.

South Korea has a long and varied coast. Along the Korea Strait and Yellow Sea, tidal flats and wetlands form beside river basins and estuaries. Some beaches in the west, such as Muchangpo Beach, are wide and flat. In Busan, sandy beaches are popular spots for tourists. Along the east coast, forested peaks seem to rise from the sea. On islands such as Yeonhwa, jagged outcrops of rock sink straight into the water.

Millions of Koreans and tourists from throughout the world visit Haeundae Beach in Busan every year.

South Korea's Geographic Features

Area: 38,502 square miles (99,720 sq km)

Highest Elevation: Mount Halla, 6,398 feet (1,950 m) above sea level

Longest Mountain Range: Taebaek Mountains, 300 miles (500 km) through North and South Korea

Lowest Elevation: Sea level along the coast

Longest River: Nakdong, 314 miles (505 km)

Largest Waterfall: Cheonjiyeon, 72 feet (22 m) high, 39 feet (12 m) wide

Largest Island: Jeju, 712 square miles (1,845 sq km)

Largest National Park: Dadohaehaesang National Marine Park, 850 square miles (2,200 sq km)

Average High Temperature: In Seoul, 35°F (2°C) in January, 84°F (29°C) in July

Average Low Temperature: In Seoul, 22°F (–6°C) in January, 71°F (22°C) in July

Average Annual Precipitation: In Seoul, 57 inches (145 cm)

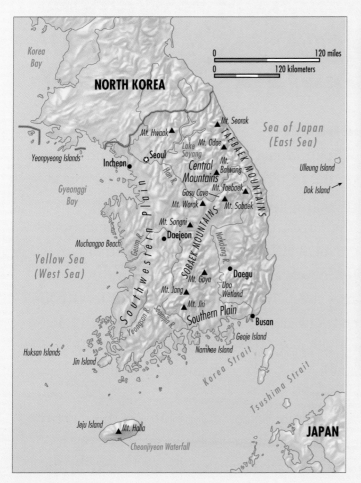

Cheonjiyeon Waterfall

Mount Hambaek in the Taebaek range is a popular destination for hikers.

Mountains and Islands

The backbone of South Korea is the Taebaek mountain range, which runs along the eastern coast of the peninsula, spreading westward through both North Korea and South Korea. The Taebaeks, the largest of the peninsula's three mountain ranges, stretch a total of 300 miles (500 km). The other ranges in Korea are the Sobaek and the Jiri Massif. Most of South Korea's mountains rise between 2,000 and 3,500 feet (600 and 1,100 meters). Hwaak, which reaches 4,817 feet (1,468 m), Balwang at 4,784 feet (1,458 m), and Jang at 4,619 feet (1,408 m) are among the tallest. Balwang is South Korea's most popular ski resort.

The mountains feature steep, sheer cliffs on the eastern side and gentle sloping inclines to the west. The country's major rivers, the Han, Nakdong, and Geum, begin in the

Taebaeks. The mountains are also a principal source of iron, coal, tungsten, fluorite, and limestone. Many of the lower mountains are covered with dense forests, which provide timber for the country.

Mount Halla, South Korea's tallest mountain, is a volcano situated on Jeju, an island off the southwest coast. It rises 6,398 feet (1,950 m) above sea level. Baengnokdam Lake fills Halla's caldera, the bowl-like formation at the top of the mountain where the volcano collapsed. The volcano has not erupted since the year 1007 and appears to be dormant.

Mount Halla and the surrounding area are protected as part of a national park.

Nearly three thousand small islands dot the seas near the southern and western coasts of South Korea. Most of the islands are unoccupied, but others have small cities to support tourist visits. Jeju Island is the largest. It is known for its beautiful vistas, scenic hiking trails, and miles of sandy beaches. For many years, Jeju has been the top vacation spot of South Korea.

In the southwest are the Huksan Islands. The largest island in this archipelago, or string of islands, is Taehuksan. It is largely unoccupied, with an observation post for botanical surveys. The islands Ulleung and Dok, in the Sea of Japan,

Millions of visitors flock to Jeju Island every year.

Dadohaehaesang National Marine Park

The largest national park in South Korea is Dadohaehaesang National Marine Park. It includes many islands and miles of coastline along the western and southern coast of South Korea. Broadleaf evergreens, such as camellias, magnolias, wild azaleas, and laurels grow on the park's islands. In all, more than 1,500 species of plants thrive there, as well as nearly 150 bird species and eleven mammal species. Island waters host 154 species of saltwater fish, a handful of reptile species, and stunning coral reef ecosystems. Endangered species protected in this park include delicate orchids in humid forestland, snakes in the wetlands, and otter and sea corals in the sea.

are the farthest from mainland South Korea. Dok Island is a matter of dispute between South Korea and Japan, with both nations claiming the island as their own.

South Korea also has territorial disputes with North Korea. Yeonpyeong is a cluster of islands in the Yellow Sea, claimed by both South and North Korea. In 2010, North Korea shelled Yeonpyeong in what they claim was a reaction to South Korea's military exercises near the border between the two nations' territorial waters.

Rivers and Lakes

South Korea's great rivers all rise in the Taebaek Mountains and tumble down to empty into the seas. The Han River begins in North Korea, passes southwest through Seoul, the capital of South Korea, and empties into the Yellow Sea at

Going Deep

Stepping into a cavern that is 4,265 feet (1,300 m) deep below a mountain does not suit everyone, but Gosu Cave attracts thousands of visitors each year. A limestone cave in Danyang County, Gosu was once a home to prehistoric humans. It maintains a constant temperature of 59 degrees Fahrenheit (15 degrees Celsius) year-round. Gosu is a geological wonder, filled with stalactites, stalagmites, cave coral, and crystals. Some of these structures resemble whale baleen or organ pipes, while others look like fuzzy swirls. Humans, however, are not Gosu's only visitors. Tourists need to keep an eye out for bats and two dozen other species of wildlife that live in the cave.

Incheon. The Han flows for a total of 319 miles (513 km), a good portion of it in North Korea. South Korea's longest river that is completely within its borders is the Nakdong, which runs 314 miles (505 km) from near Taebaek City to Busan, where it empties into the Korea Strait.

Rapid industrialization has caused most of South Korea's rivers to become heavily polluted. The Four Major Rivers Restoration Project is under way to restore the Han, Nakdong, Geum, and Yeongsan Rivers. The massive project, expected to cost US$18 billion, is intended to reduce pollution in the four major rivers, fourteen tributaries, and more than one thousand streams.

South Korea has few natural lakes. More common are reservoirs, or artificial lakes, which are created when dams are constructed. Lake Soyang, the nation's largest lake, is 635 feet (194 m) long and was formed by a hydroelectric dam.

Hot Summers, Cold Winters

South Korea's climate is temperate with four distinct seasons. Spring is mild, with warm days and cold nights. The summers are hot, wet, and steamy. Autumn brings crisp days, drier weather, and an abundance of fall colors. Winters are long, cold, and dry.

The East Asian monsoon, which in South Korea is called *jangma*, affects the nation. A monsoon is a powerful wind system that reverses directions based upon the season. In South Korea during the spring and summer, monsoon winds carry wet air from the Indian and Pacific Oceans, bringing abundant rain and high humidity. The winter monsoon brings cold, dry winds from the north.

Maples and other trees beautify South Korea with bright reds, oranges, and yellows each fall.

Looking at South Korea's Cities

South Korea's largest city is its capital, Seoul, which had a population of 10,349,312 in 2013. The nation's second-largest city, Busan (below), has a population of 3,678,555. Busan is a sprawling city on the southeastern tip of the Korean Peninsula. It is the site of the nation's largest port and one of the busiest seaports in the world. A popular tourist site, the city boasts several museums, including the Busan Marine Natural History Museum, the Museum of Art, and the Busanpo Folk Museum. Busan is also known for its fish markets. The largest one, called Jagalchi, is popular with tourists.

Incheon, with a population of 2,628,000, is South Korea's third-largest city. A major port, it is situated where the Han River pours into the Yellow Sea. Located near Seoul, it is also the site of South Korea's largest international airport. Korea's only Chinatown is in Incheon, and the city hosts festivals featuring Chinese traditions such as dragon dances.

Daegu (above), the nation's fourth-largest city, is home to 2,566,540 people. It lies along the Geumho River in the southeastern part of the country. The site has been occupied since prehistoric days and was officially named in 757 CE. Today, Daegu is a major manufacturing city, particularly of textiles, metals, and machinery. It is also an active robotics center with a large technology complex. Roughly forty traditional outdoor markets occupy streets throughout the city. The large Seomun Market has ten thousand merchants, and more than 70 percent of the shops sell clothing.

In Seoul, in the northwest, temperatures reach an average of 84°F (29°C) on summer days. At the opposite end of South Korea, Jeju Island experiences similar temperatures. The highest temperature ever recorded in South Korea was 104°F (40°C) in Daegu on August 1, 1940. The lowest temperature ever recorded was –27°F (–33°C) in Yangpyeong on January 5, 1981.

On average, about 40 inches (100 centimeters) of rain falls each year across South Korea. Drought is cyclical, and a very dry year occurs about every eight years. About 60 percent of all precipitation falls between June and September.

An average of about three typhoons, the Asian equivalent of hurricanes, strike South Korea each year. The typhoons bring heavy rainfall, which often leads to flooding. In 1984, record-breaking floods cost 190 people their lives and left more than two hundred thousand people homeless.

July and August are Seoul's rainiest months, with average rainfall amounting to nearly 30 inches (76 cm).

CHAPTER 3

Wonderful Wildlife

IT IS A CHILLY NOVEMBER MORNING, AND KIM JIN-young's biology class is taking part in a bird census in the eastern province of North Gyeongsang. The students are divided into pairs, and each pair has a list of species to look for. Kim and his partner are lucky. They spot a scaly-sided merganser shortly after arriving in their designated area. Kim snaps a photo with his cell phone and sends the shot to his teacher.

The census is important. Migrating bird populations in South Korea are rapidly declining because of habitat loss, pollution, and climate change. Today, shorebirds such as the spoon-billed sandpiper and the black-tailed godwit are rarely seen. The census will be used to convince the government to dedicate resources to preserving wetland habitats.

Birds of a Feather

South Korea is home to nearly five hundred species of birds. Many migrating birds winter there in the tidal wetlands and

Opposite: **Twenty species of gulls make their home along the South Korean coast.**

freshwater marshes. Ducks, geese, and swans are plentiful. Mute swans, whooper swans, and tundra swans visit yearly. South Korea's wading birds include crested ibises, herons, egrets, and cranes.

Thirty-two species of birds of prey are native to South Korea. These include hawks, eagles, falcons, kites, and buzzards. Ospreys, Steller's sea eagles and white-tailed eagles are large, fish-eating species, while the smaller peregrine falcons hunt other birds. Japanese sparrowhawks and several falcon species feed on birds caught in flight. Chinese goshawks are frequently seen living in or near ponds or streams, where they feed mainly on frogs and lizards.

Ospreys have small hooks or spines on the bottom of their feet. This allows them to grip slippery fish.

In South Korean forests, woodpeckers tap noisily against tree trunks in the hope of finding a host of insects. Other forest birds add their songs to the woodpeckers' drumlike drilling. Larks, bulbuls, kinglets, and wrens sing as they hunt for insects, berries, or seeds. South Korea also has a wide variety of warblers, known for distinctive songs.

Mammals

Rodents make up 40 percent of South Korea's mammal species. Red squirrels have a mane of long red hair standing straight up along their backs, making them appear startled. Siberian flying squirrels are tree dwellers that soar from branch to branch among forest treetops. Scurrying along forest and meadow floors are field mice, hedgehogs, and rats.

About one in five Korean mammal species is a bat. The nation is home to tiny birdlike noctules, whiskered bats, and pipistrelles. Greater horseshoe bats stick close to home as they hunt for moths in the night sky. Eastern long-fingered bats and Serotine bats are plentiful, but little tube-nosed bats and Kobayashi's bats are rare.

Species in Danger: Asiatic Black Bear

Also known as the moon bear, the Asiatic black bear is a medium-sized bear noted for the crescent-shaped white patch on its chest. Asiatic black bears had almost disappeared from South Korea because of hunting and the cutting down of the forests where they live. To restore the population, twenty-seven bear cubs were imported from Russia and North Korea, and released in Jirisan National Park. As a result of this restoration program, several cubs have been born in the wild.

Many species of carnivores, or meat eaters, live in South Korea. The biggest predator is the rare Amur leopard, which was once hunted for its spotted fur. There are also red foxes, gray wolves, raccoon dogs, and badgers. Mountain weasels, least weasels, and otters live in the wilds by Korea's rivers and streams. These creatures prey on rodents, birds, reptiles, and a range of herbivores.

The Amur Tiger

No one has seen an Amur tiger, also known as a Korean tiger, in the wild for many years, but its importance in Korean culture cannot be overstated. The tiger is found in Korean mythology and folklore. Traditionally, the Korean people believe the tiger serves as a guardian of the people, driving away evil spirits. Scientists have found that the Amur tiger and the Siberian tiger, which live in Russia, are the same species. As long as Siberian tigers survive, Korea's national symbol will stay alive.

The most common herbivores are deer and gorals. Siberian musk deer are small and nocturnal. They have two tusklike teeth that grow throughout their life. Sika deer and water deer are found throughout the mainland. Long-tailed gorals are an endangered species. Relatives of goats, gorals are found only in the Taebaek Mountains and the DMZ.

In the Sea

Many different kinds of animal species live in the waters off Korea. Green sea turtles swim in shallow seas, munching on sea grasses. Huge leatherback turtles feed on jellyfish, while

Sika deer flourish in South Korea's densely forested areas.

loggerhead sea turtles eat almost anything they find, including jellies, sponges, corals, sea anemones, and starfish. Sei whales, gray whales, spinner dolphins, and porpoises swim Korea's calm waters. Spinner dolphins are acrobatic. They leap from the water, spin around rapidly, and then plunge back into the sea.

Seals and sea lions are found in both the Yellow Sea and the Sea of Japan. Northern fur seals, common in the Sea of Japan, are considered vulnerable species due to overhunting for their fur. Steller sea lions swim in all waters around South Korea. Harbor seals and spotted seals can be found off eastern port cities.

Spinner dolphins often do a whole series of acrobatics, sometimes performing fourteen leaps in a row.

The Ecorium

South Korea's Ecorium at the National Ecology Center in Seocheon, along the west coast, is an educational and research center that gives visitors a firsthand look at many different kinds of ecosystems. The Ecorium consists of a series of connected domes, each housing a specific climate zone, including a tropical rain forest, a polar zone, and a dry tropical region. This allows visitors to experience a wide variety of ecosystems all in one place.

Beware!

South Korea has a number of animals that can be dangerous to humans. High on the list is the wild boar, which is strong, fast, and aggressive. It is also important to watch out for deadly insects. Asian giant hornets live in large trees and might bite people who get too close. The sting is potent and too many stings can cause death. Slithering through mountain forests and along streams, Amur vipers and Ussuri mamushi snakes cannot kill an adult human, but their venom can be deadly for children. These are hissing snakes that warn before they strike, so hikers can usually avoid problems. Not as easy to avoid are jellyfish. More than two thousand jellyfish stings are reported every year. Most occur during warm months when Koreans head to the beach, and jellyfish arrive in local seas.

Trees, Mushrooms, and Flowers

South Korea boasts a wide variety of deciduous trees, which lose their leaves in autumn. Geojesu namu has pale tan bark

The geojesu namu is part of the birch tree family, a type of tree that is found in many temperate areas in the Northern Hemisphere.

that peels off like paper. Geojesu namu produces seedpods that look like pinecones. Chosenia is another native tree with peeling bark. It has long leaves and small flowers. Korea has species of larches, oaks, maples, and elms. In early spring, Korean villagers trudge up the mountains to maple groves, where they tap the maples for the sap, which they drink. The sap is believed to provide a wide range of health benefits.

Among South Korea's evergreens are magnolias, camphor trees, Manchurian firs, and pines. Magnolias are prized for their deep green foliage and soft white blossoms. Camphor produces a substance that is used in food, incense, and medicine. It also makes a great insect repellent. Japanese red pine, another South Korea native, is a skinny tree with a puff of needles at the top and small cones.

Mushrooms grow throughout the mountain ranges. Most are edible, but a few make people sick. It takes an expert to know which are toxic. Parasol mushrooms, shaggy ink caps, and puffballs grow wild and are safe to eat. Mangtae mushrooms have orange netting that covers the lower half of the stem. Lion's mane mushrooms grow in and on trees, as do bearded hedgehog mushrooms. The shapes and colors of these wild mushrooms look nothing like the varieties sold in American supermarkets.

Wildflowers and herbs color the mountainside in spring and thrive in the damp wetlands near the coast. In the mountains and foothills, wildflowers bloom throughout the year. Pink camellias blossom in the winter and two other times during the year. Brilliant yellow sansuyu announces the arrival of spring, along with wild azaleas, vivid pink phlox, and blue-and-white columbine. Summer meadows are filled with Korean daisies and red bleeding hearts. Hillside shrubs sprout delicate hibiscus blossoms, the national flower of South Korea. Autumn brings lavender hues of gaksichwi and fluttering yellow-flowered reeds.

The National Flower

From July to October, bright pink rose of Sharon, a type of hibiscus, blooms throughout South Korea. In Korea, this flower is called *mugunghwa*. The word *mugung* means immortality. Historically, the plant's leaves have been brewed as herbal tea, and the petals were eaten. The bright pink blossom is often featured in traditional Korean paintings.

Conservation and the Environment

South Korea is a densely populated country that industrialized relatively late. With industrialization came a variety of environmental issues. Seoul is particularly affected by air pollution. The government has enacted a number of conservation laws to limit air and water pollution and preserve the nation's plant and animal diversity. In 2000, the Ministry of Environment began an extensive program to protect the environment and promote green, environmentally friendly development.

Government plans include rewards for burning less coal and oil, which produce a lot of pollutants such as carbon dioxide. The government encourages the use of natural gas and solar power, which are cleaner. The South Korean government has an agreement with China to reduce emissions since winds from China carry pollutants into South Korea.

South Korea has a large population, so it uses a lot of water. The government has created the Four Major Rivers Restoration Project, which includes building dams with small hydroelectric power plants that produce cheaper, cleaner electricity. But the lakes these dams create will cause a serious environmental impact on wetlands and river habitats. Although buffer zones to protect animal species are planned, conservationists are concerned about the effects of the Four Rivers program.

South Korea's national parks and preserves cover slightly less than 7 percent of the country's land. The largest mountainous park is Jirisan National Park in the southern region.

Dadohaehaesang is the largest marine park, while Halla occupies a large portion of Jeju Island. Gyeongju National Park is the country's only historic park. It covers the historical site that was the foundation of the ancient Silla dynasty.

Several of the parks have UNESCO World Heritage status, meaning the United Nations (UN) has designated them as having particular scientific, educational, historical, or cultural significance. Seoraksan, the northernmost park, is a biosphere reserve and home to many rare plants and animals. Bukhansan, north of Seoul, is a mountain park popular with hikers. To protect the environment, trails in Bukhansan are open on a rotational basis, allowing areas to recover from human contact. While all national parks are open to tourists, some are remote and rarely visited.

A Vital Wetland

The Upo Wetland is a string of natural wetlands, swamps, and shallow ponds near the Nakdong River in southern South Korea. The area is home to 342 endangered or threatened species. The rarest plant in Upo is the prickly lotus, and the rarest bird is the black-faced spoonbill. Migrating birds make temporary homes in this freshwater wetland. Sweet flag and Sangigarae plants feed on nutrients that might pollute the water, keeping Upo's fresh water clean. The fish that live in the wetland include snakehead, crucian carp, and catfish, which provide food for the local population, although only a handful of people are allowed to harvest fish from Upo's waters.

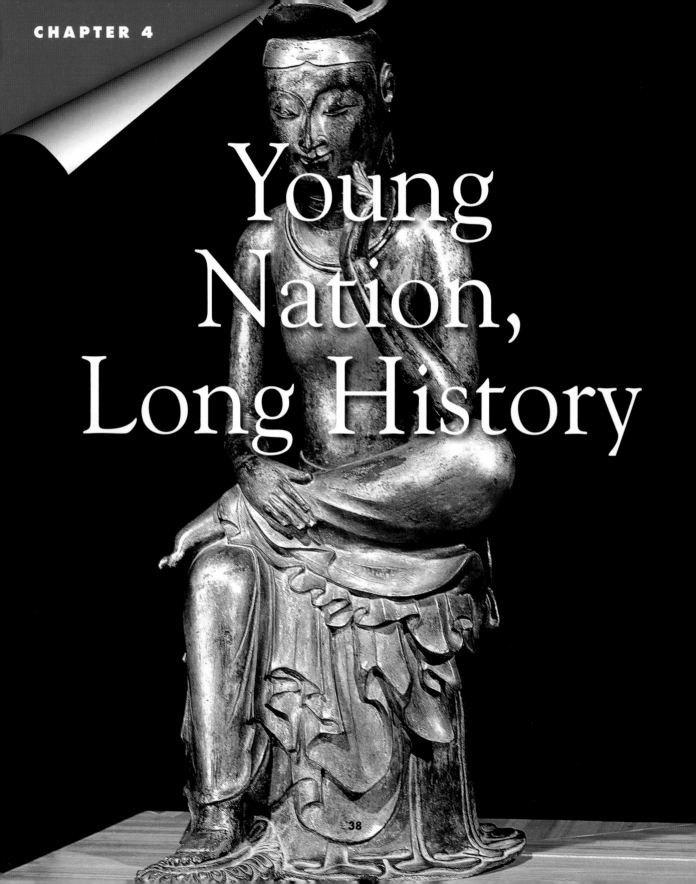

CHAPTER 4

Young Nation, Long History

38

SOME THIRTY-TWO THOUSAND YEARS AGO, HUMANS entered the Korean Peninsula and established settlements. They lived in caves in Korea's many mountains, fished the streams, and gathered nuts, berries, and fruit to eat. These settlers came from central and northern Asia. The settlements gave rise to different tribes, connected by family and culture. Rival tribes battled over territories that provided the best opportunities for finding food and shelter.

By 300 BCE, the Gojoseon people had become the most powerful of the tribal groups. Living in the north, they came into regular conflict with the Chinese. Constant raids by the tribe led to China's Han dynasty invading the north in 108 BCE. The Chinese quickly established four fortresses, which served as military stations and trading posts for the next four hundred years.

Opposite: **A statue of the Buddha dating to the 600s** CE

The Three Kingdoms

Tribal bonds led to the development of three kingdoms: Koguryo in the north, Paekche in the southwest, and Silla in the southeast. In addition, the small confederation of Gaya rose as an alliance of tribes along the Nakdong River. All three kingdoms thrived on agriculture, with the main crop being rice. All three also looked to China as a cultural model. Only Gaya allied itself with Japan's culture. Buddhism became the religion of the kingdoms. Despite having so much in common, the three constantly battled one another.

This vase was found in the tomb of King Michu of Silla, who died in 284.

The largest of the kingdoms was Koguryo (37 BCE–668 CE). Koguryo had a well-organized monarchy and military and eventually expanded to cover an area stretching from north of the Amnok River to more than halfway down the Korean Peninsula. During the Koguryo reign, a one-hundred-volume history of the kingdom was produced. The kingdom's capital fell to the Chinese in 342 CE.

Paekche (18 BCE–660 CE) arose beside the Han River in the area near what is now Seoul. Under the reign of Geunchogo, who ruled from 346 to 375, Paekche developed into a strong state with an active trade program with China.

Silla was small but well organized. The kingdom developed the Hwarang, a volunteer youth militia. The young army trained in war strategy, committed to loyalty to their ruler, family, and friends, in that order. They also swore never to retreat from battle but to avoid killing unless necessary. Silla became a cultural and religious center, building temples, such as the Hwangnyongsa (Temple of the Illustrious Dragon), and a massive pagoda that is said to have impressed even the Chinese.

By the middle of the seventh century, Koguryo was suffering from weak leadership and many years of war with China.

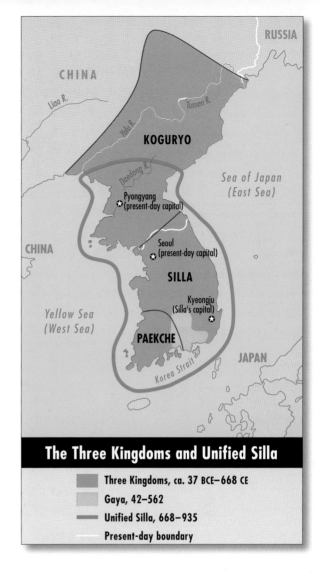

The Three Kingdoms and Unified Silla

- ▧ Three Kingdoms, ca. 37 BCE–668 CE
- ▨ Gaya, 42–562
- ▬ Unified Silla, 668–935
- ┄ Present-day boundary

Kongfuzi (551–479 BCE), known as Confucius in the West, was a Chinese philosopher whose teachings became the educational foundation for many young men in Korea through periods when China exerted influence over Korea.

Confucius wrote *Analects*, in which he voiced his fundamental beliefs. Confucius arranged the world according to important bonds and their defining quality. Many relationships and hierarchies in Korea today continue to follow this order. The five bonds are between friends, based on trust; between young and old, based on respect; between husband and wife, based on a division of duties; between father and son, based on intimacy; and between kings and ministers, based on loyalty.

In 612, the Emperor Yang-ti of China's Sui dynasty invaded Koguryo with more than one million soldiers. Koguryo's military held their positions against the Sui army for several months, and the Sui troops eventually retreated.

Unified Silla

Silla had learned valuable lessons from its larger neighbor. The kingdom became allies with the Tang of China. When the Tang needed help, Silla came to their aid. So when Silla wanted help to defeat Paekche and Koguryo, it turned to the Tang. In the 660s, Silla took control of the entire Korean Peninsula. Korea changed from a string of tribal bonds to a unified nation under King Munmu.

The Unified Silla dynasty (668–935) had its capital in Kyeongju, where art and architecture reached a high level.

Buddhism was the state religion. The dynasty made many advances in art and science, including the study of astronomy at the Cheomseongdae Observatory.

The Rise of Koryo

By 935, Silla's dynasty was weakening, and Koguryo saw the opportunity to emerge from Silla's rule. Koguryo stepped into the lead and changed its name to Koryo. The Koryo dynasty ruled from 935 to 1392.

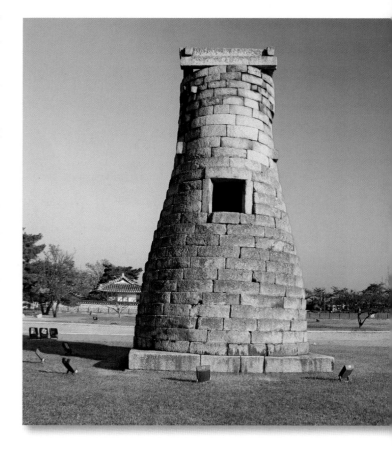

One of the oldest surviving astronomical observatories in the world, Cheomseongdae was built in the 600s.

The Koryo rulers developed a relationship with the Mongol Empire, which spread across much of Asia. The Koreans learned about growing and processing cotton from the Mongols. They also advanced their medical knowledge. But the Mongols demanded that Koryo pay tribute to the Mongol leader and marry Koryo princes to Mongol princesses. The rulers of the Mongol Empire believed this would ensure Koryo loyalty to the Mongols. The Koryo fought Mongol rule, but without success.

The Hermit Kingdom

By the late 1300s, the Koryo dynasty was struggling with internal political problems. On the surface, the

Mongol Empire ruled Koryo, but that empire was also on the wane. In 1392, an army general named Yi Song-gye ousted the Koryo king and started the Joseon dynasty.

A primary goal of the Joseon dynasty was to reduce the power of Buddhism in Korea. Temples were destroyed, monastery lands were taken over, and students were taught the rules of Confucianism. Social groups became more rigid. A

Changdeokgung Palace in Seoul was built during the Joseon dynasty.

Sejong the Great

In 1418, Sejong (1397–1450) became the fourth Joseon king. Under his rule, Korea entered a golden era, and Sejong became known as Sejong the Great. Interest in culture and the arts expanded. University scholars developed hangul, the Korean alphabet that is still used today. Sejong's interest in science and inventions led to the development of astronomical maps, celestial globes, rain gauges, and water clocks. Under the king's guidance, doctors produced a medical dictionary and an eighty-five-volume medical encyclopedia. Long before Gutenberg developed movable type in Germany, Sejong's printers invented movable type in hangul for producing farming and medical manuals.

man's status and occupation became more closely linked to his social status. Women were pronounced inferior, and males dominated everything from education to politics to the home. Korea began a period of isolationism, avoiding relationships with neighboring countries and refusing trade agreements with outsiders. As a result, Korea earned the nickname the Hermit Kingdom.

Battling Outside Forces

In the 1590s, Japan invaded Korea as a stepping-stone to invading China. Korean admiral Yi Sun-sin wanted to turn back the Japanese navy, but he had few ships. He designed ironclad "turtle ships," which worked well against the Japanese invaders. In the Battle of Myeongnyang, Yi had 13 ships to

Admiral Yi Sun-sin became a hero for his victories against the Japanese.

Japan's 133. Yi's ships sank 33 Japanese vessels and turned the Japanese back from Korean shores. In the end, China helped Korea repel the Japanese, but the war devastated Korea. Many towns and villages were razed and crops destroyed.

Turtle Ships

The *keobukseon*, or turtle ship, was the first ironclad warship, invented in the 1500s under the guidance of Admiral Yi Sun-sin. The ships measured 112 feet (34 m) long, 21 feet (6 m) high, and 34 feet (10 m) wide. The bow featured a dragon's head, and the stern had a turtle's tail. Rowers along both sides propelled the boat, while cannons fired iron cannonballs through the dragon's "mouth." Rowers, gunners, archers, and cannons were hidden by thick iron cladding. Those within the ship could see out, but those attacking could not see into the turtle ships. With a small fleet of turtle ships Admiral Yi defeated the larger Japanese navy.

In the 1700s, some Western ideas began to seep into Korea through its ties with China. In 1783, Korean Yi Seung-hun converted to Catholicism and brought his religion with him to Korea from China. Christianity was alien to Koreans, who had followed Buddhist and Confucian philosophies for centuries. Some Koreans found Christianity appealing and converted. By 1791, the persecution of Catholics had begun. In 1839, 130 Christians were executed, and in the late 1860s, Joseon king Yi Myeong-bok ordered nearly eight thousand Christians executed.

The nineteenth century brought new conflicts to Korea. While Korea tried to reject all efforts from other countries to enter into trade and political arrangements with it, European nations established solid relationships with China. Western nations also pressed Korean leaders to open their ports. Russia and the United States tried to force Korea to accept trade agreements. The United States pushed its view by sending warships. Skirmishes between Korea and the United States resulted in the U.S. occupation of Kanghwa Island, off the Korean mainland. Japan also stepped up pressure on Korea, and Korea finally opened three ports for trade under the Treaty of Kanghwa in 1876.

European missionaries such as Karl Gützlaff of Germany spread Christianity in Korea and other parts of Asia during the 1800s.

Changing Times

Gradually, the country began to modernize. Some Koreans were fed up with the slow pace of change, however, and in 1884, there was a revolt called the Gapsin Coup. The rebels' victory was short-lived. As the army rebelled, China sent in troops to support the Korean king, Yi Myeong-bok. China put down the revolt three days after it started.

The port at Incheon opened up international trade in the late 1800s.

But Korea continued to face angry citizens. Poor peasant farmers were treated badly and taxed more heavily than other people. By 1894, the peasants began protesting and demanding reform in what is called the Donghak Uprising. The weak Korean government could not handle the uprising on its own and asked the Chinese for help. Japan also sent in troops.

Although the Donghak rebels soon ended their uprising, China and Japan remained in conflict over control of Korea, and the Sino-Japanese War broke out. By 1895, China wanted peace. China recognized Korea's independence, but Japan did not give in so easily. A plot by the Japanese ended in the murder of Empress Myeongseong, usually known as Queen Min. Japan's government viewed Queen Min as an obstacle to its efforts to increase Japanese influence in Korea because the queen favored ties with Russia.

Japanese forces construct a bridge in Korea during the Sino-Japanese War.

In 1897, the Joseon dynasty changed its name to the Korean Empire, but that dynasty would be short-lived. Japan had not given up its desire to keep Korea as its own.

Japan Takes Over

The Japan-Korea Treaty of 1905 made Korea a protectorate of Japan. This meant that on the surface, Korea still had its own ruler—King Gojong—but Japan controlled the government. Gojong tried to show Korea's independence by sending representatives to a peace conference in The Hague, Netherlands. Korea's representatives hoped to present Gojong's position that Korea should rule itself without Japan's interference, but Korea's representatives were not allowed to attend. Clearly, other nations no longer recognized Korea as a separate country. Two years later, Gojong stepped down from the throne, and his son Sunjong became the new emperor. In 1910, Japan annexed Korea as a colony.

Korean citizens hated Japan's rule. Rebels organized into protest groups. In 1919, the former emperor Gojong died suddenly, and Koreans believed the death was mysterious. Peaceful demonstrations filled Korea's streets, only to be violently crushed by Japanese soldiers and police. A Korean declaration of independence was read at a rally on March 1, 1919, so the demonstrations became known as the March First Movement. Although the protests failed, some change did occur. Korea was allowed to form a provisional government, and some Koreans formed an armed militia.

At the start of World War II, Japan used Korea as a pathway for invading China. Thousands of Korean men were forced to enlist in the Japanese army. Women and the elderly worked in plants to produce Japanese weapons, planes, and ships. In

Freedom Fighter

Ryu Kwan-sun (1904–1920) was only sixteen years old when she helped organize the March 1, 1919, protest for independence. The demonstration was nonviolent, but the ruling Japanese reacted brutally. Japanese authorities killed protest organizers and arrested demonstrators, including Ryu. Ryu was tortured for several days, and then put in prison. She was tried, found guilty, and given a three-year prison sentence. Ryu died from the torture she suffered. About 7,500 demonstrators died during the March First Movement protests, and 45,000 were arrested. Although independence would not come for another twenty-five years, Ryu Kwan-sun is still honored for her sacrifice.

the late 1930s, Japanese authorities forced Korean citizens to change their names to Japanese names. Koreans went without food, heating fuel, and medicines so that Japanese troops could have provisions. The Koreans were angry at their treatment, but with a war beginning, it was not a time for rebellion.

A Divided Korea

In August 1945, the United States dropped atomic bombs on Hiroshima and Nagasaki, Japan. World War II was about to end. In southern Korea, the Japanese military surrendered to the U.S. Army; in northern Korea, they surrendered to the army of the Soviet Union. The United States and the Soviet Union (a large communist nation in eastern Europe and central Asia that split apart into more than a dozen countries, including Russia, in 1991) were allies during the war, but that soon changed. U.S. and Soviet officials could not agree on how to replace Japanese rule with an independent Korean government. So Korea was divided at the 38th parallel. The Soviet Union occupied the northern part of the peninsula, and the United States the southern part.

In 1948, the two parts of Korea formed separate governments. The Democratic People's Republic of Korea was established in the north, with its capital at Pyongyang. The Republic of Korea was established in the south, with its capital at Seoul. North Korea, like the Soviet Union and China, was communist. The leaders of South Korea, like those of the United States, opposed communism. With the support of the United States, Syngman Rhee, a Korean with a strong dislike for communism, became the president of South Korea. Rhee,

U.S. officials believed, would hold off any attempts by communist North Korea to take over South Korea.

Both Korean governments wanted to control the entire peninsula. In 1950, the two Koreas went to war when North Korean troops invaded South Korea. American and UN forces rushed in to help South Korea, while China supported North Korea. The Korean War was brutal. Three million Koreans, one million Chinese, and fifty-four thousand American troops died. Many factories were destroyed, and one-third of the homes in Korea were damaged. By 1953, the two sides had battled to roughly the same line as where they had started, along the 38th parallel. That year, an armistice, or an agreement to stop fighting, was approved. The Demilitarized Zone (DMZ) was created to form a buffer between the two nations.

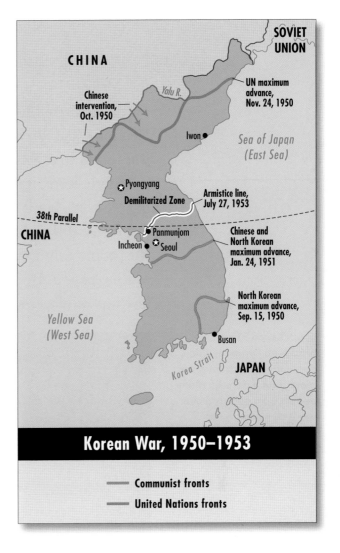

Korean War, 1950–1953

— Communist fronts
— United Nations fronts

The Postwar Years

Young South Korea went through some unpleasant growing pains. Rhee's party dominated the legislature. Although under the South Korean constitution, presidents were limited to two terms, an amendment was passed that allowed Rhee to be elected to a third term. When Rhee was elected to a fourth term in 1960, many people believed there had been election fraud. Student demonstrators filled the streets. Rhee was forced to resign, and he fled to Hawaii.

South Korea revised its constitution and formed a new government, but it did not last long. In 1961, a military coup put General Park Chung-hee in power. Park initially allowed the people political freedom, but he became more of a dictator as time passed. By 1972, political freedom was gone. Martial law was in place, meaning that the military rather than the

South Korea's first president, Syngman Rhee, dominated the country for more than a decade. Many people who opposed him were arrested.

Massive demonstrations took place against martial law in the early 1980s.

police was in charge of keeping the peace. During these years, industry grew rapidly in South Korea.

In 1979, Park was assassinated by his own security chief while at dinner. General Chun Doo-hwan took control. When students demonstrated in the streets, Korean soldiers and police put down the protest. In Gwangju, the army killed hundreds of people. Political activity was banned, and colleges were closed.

Once again, the government revised the constitution. General Chun won election to a seven-year presidential term the following year, and the government ended martial law.

In 1987, South Korea revised its constitution again. After years of military rule, South Korea finally held its first truly democratic elections that December. Roh Tae-woo was elected president, and when he took office in 1988 South Korea had its first peaceful transfer of power.

Working for Change

Kim Dae-jung (near left) spent most of his life trying to change South Korea's political system. Beginning in the 1950s, he worked as an activist trying to get the country to become more democratic. In the following decades, he frequently spoke out against South Korea's repressive government. Because of his activities, he was arrested several times and sentenced to a long jail term. After he was freed, he continued to speak out in opposition to the nation's rulers.

Kim ran for president in 1987 and 1992, but lost both times. Finally, in 1997, he won the presidential election. As president, he began a "sunshine policy" toward North Korea. He encouraged improved relations between the two countries and held a historic summit meeting with North Korean leader Kim Jong Il (above

right). Because of Kim's efforts in support of democracy in South Korea and peace with North Korea, he received the Nobel Peace Prize in 2000.

Recent Times

In the early years of its democracy, South Korea struggled over charges of corruption and incompetence among its leaders. Both Roh and the president before him, Chun Doo-hwan, were convicted of corruption. In addition, business leaders, including the heads of the car companies Daewoo and Hyundai, faced trials for embezzlement and bribing government officials.

In 1997, Kim Dae-jung, who had long opposed the rulers of South Korea, was elected president. Kim tried to improve relations with North Korea. In 2000, Kim met North Korea's leader Kim Jong Il at a summit meeting. This was the first meeting between leaders of the two Koreas. As a result of the summit meeting, South Korea agreed to give amnesty to

Family Reunions

After more than forty-five years of division, South Koreans were finally given an opportunity to see family members who had been restricted north of the Demilitarized Zone after the Korean War. The first reunion for one hundred South Koreans took place in 2000. Later reunions have been few, with a total of just seventeen thousand people visiting on seventeen occasions. During each of those reunions, South Koreans had to head north, because North Koreans are not allowed to visit South Korea. Eighty thousand South Koreans have signed up for the visits, but the Ministry of Unification believes at least half of those people have died waiting for permission.

3,500 North Korean prisoners, and the first reunion was held between North and South Korean relatives since they had been separated by the DMZ in 1953. Both sides also agreed to work toward the reunification of Korea as a single country.

Minor incidents continue to cause problems between North and South Korea. In 2002, a group of North Koreans defected to South Korea. They brought news of famine and political oppression in North Korea. Three months later, a battle between North Korean and South Korean naval vessels took place along the disputed sea border. In 2010, a South Korean warship exploded near North Korean waters. It was later determined that it had been hit by a North Korean torpedo. Despite such incidents, there are bright spots in the relationship between the two Koreas, and 2007 saw passenger trains traveling across the DMZ for the first time.

CHAPTER 5

A Strong Republic

T HE REPUBLIC OF KOREA IS A YOUNG NATION, FORMED only in 1948. In the first few decades of its existence, it suffered through war, military coups, and dictatorships. It was not until 1987 that South Korea had a democratic presidential election.

Through the nation's many years of turmoil, the South Korean constitution has been rewritten several times. Today, the constitution defines a three-branch government structure. It limits the powers of the president in the executive branch, establishes a strong legislature, and provides for an independent judicial branch.

The Executive Branch

South Korea selects its president by a nationwide popular vote. Presidents may serve one five-year term. This prevents any one person from becoming too powerful for too long a

Opposite: **A woman's two children help her cast her vote in a 2014 election in Seoul.**

President Park meets with her cabinet, or advisers, in March 2013. Cabinet members help the president stay informed and make difficult decisions.

time. If the president dies or becomes disabled, the nation's prime minister or a member of the cabinet serves as president until a new election is held. In 2012, South Korea elected its first female president, Park Geun-hye. She is the daughter of former leader Park Chung-hee.

The President: Park Geun-hye

South Korea's first female president, Park Geun-hye (1952–) may have inherited her political savvy. She is the daughter of former South Korean president Park Chung-hee, who served from 1961 to 1979. Park Geun-hye was appointed vice-chairperson of the Grand National Party in 1998 and was elected to the National Assembly that same year. In 2004, she became the leader of the Grand National Party. As president, Park is concerned with issues such as economic growth.

The president has five main jobs. He or she is the head of state, representing South Korea in the government and in foreign relations. Presidents perform specific duties: receiving foreign diplomats or leaders, distributing awards and honors, and granting pardons to criminals. Presidents also run the country, enforce laws, and direct the cabinet. Just as the U.S. president is commander in chief of the U.S. military, South Korea's president is the commander of his or her nation's military. The president also proposes laws to the legislature.

The cabinet consists of fifteen to thirty advisers who assist the president in running South Korea. The president appoints a prime minister, who supervises the cabinet ministries. Each cabinet minister is in charge of a different area, such as the environment, justice, or foreign affairs.

World Diplomat

Ban Ki-moon always knew he wanted to be a diplomat. In 2004, he became South Korea's foreign minister and frequently had to deal with relations between North and South Korea. By this time, he had already spent some time working at the United Nations (UN), an international organization that works to promote peace and cooperation around the world. Ban became the secretary general of the UN in 2007. As the leader of the UN, Ban has tried to help starving people in the African nation of Sudan; to end the nuclear threat in Iran; and to convince countries around the world to combat climate change. In 2013, *Forbes* magazine listed him thirty-second on its list of the most powerful people in the world.

On April 16, 2014, a South Korea ferry accident caused the deaths of nearly three hundred people. Many who died were children on a school trip. South Korea's prime minister, Chung Hong-won, resigned as anger swept through the Korean people over the government's poor handling of the accident and recovery efforts.

The Legislature

South Korea has a one-house legislature called the National Assembly. This legislature is made up of 300 lawmakers, each serving four-year terms. Of the 300 members, 246 are chosen by popular vote from designated districts. Another 54 mem-

The National Assembly meets in a large, fan-shaped room.

Supporters cheered when they learned that Park Geun-hye had won the presidential election in 2012. Park represents the New Frontier Party.

bers are given seats depending on the political party they represent. The mix of 54 members depends on how well a party has done in the most recent election. In order to earn a seat, a political party must have a minimum of 3 percent of the national vote.

Members of the National Assembly must be twenty-five years old and live in the electoral district they serve. Members attend two types of legislative sessions: regular and special. Regular sessions are held from September to December and can last no longer than one hundred days. Special sessions may be called by the president or by 25 percent of the members of the legislature. A special session can last for no more than thirty days. A majority of the members must attend a session for a vote on any proposed bill, and the bill is passed if more than half of those voting approve it.

According to the constitution, the National Assembly is given the power to initiate, discuss, and pass laws. It must approve the national budget and foreign policy matters. Only the National Assembly can enter into war, station Korean troops in other countries, or allow foreign military on South Korean soil.

The National Assembly also has the right to impeach the president if the president is believed to have broken the law. An impeachment proceeding is like a trial, and it happens only if a majority of members votes for impeachment. For a president to be removed from office due to impeachment requires a two-thirds vote of the entire National Assembly, with all members expected to be present.

Men in South Korea are required to serve at least twenty-one months in the military.

The National Anthem

The lyrics of South Korea's national anthem, "Aegukka" ("The Patriotic Song"), were written by Yun Chi-ho, and the music was written by Ahn Eak-tai. It was adopted as the national anthem in August 1948. According to legend, the lyrics were written for a ceremony at Seoul's Independence Gate in 1896. The music was written in 1935.

English translation

Until that day when Mt. Baekdu is worn away,
and the East Sea's waters run dry,
God protect and preserve our country!
Refrain:
Hibiscus and three thousand ri
full of splendid mountains and rivers;
Koreans, to the Korean way, stay always true!
As the pine atop Namsan Peak stands firm,

unchanged through wind and frost,
as if wrapped in armor, so shall our resilient spirit.
Refrain:
The Autumn skies are void and vast, high and cloudless;
the bright moon is like our heart, undivided and true.
Refrain:
With this spirit and this mind, let us give all loyalty,
in suffering or in joy, to the country's love.

Seoul: The Capital City

Seoul, the capital of South Korea, is by far the nation's largest city, with a population of 10,349,312. The city has a long history. The site had been occupied for thousands of years before Seoul first became a capital city in 1394, during the Joseon dynasty. When the city was made a capital, an 11-mile-long (18 km) wall was built to protect it. Some of this wall still stands.

Today, Seoul is a bustling city, the business, financial, and educational heart of South Korea. The city is filled with high-rise apartment buildings and office towers. It is a center for high-tech industries and electronics production. Publishing and food production are also important businesses there.

Seoul attracts more than twelve million visitors a year. They come to see sites such as Changdeokgung, one of the five grand palaces built during the Joseon dynasty. Many people visit the National Museum of Korea, which displays artifacts from throughout Korean history, the National Folk Museum, and the Seoul Museum of Art. Others visit Lotte World, the world's largest indoor theme park, or Namdaemun Market, which includes thousands of shops.

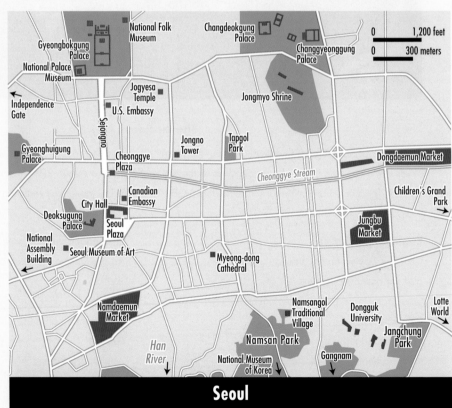

Seoul

The Judicial Branch

The South Korean judiciary is made up of all the courts, judges, and prosecuting attorneys of the country. The courts hear trials and lawsuits about civil matters, crimes, and electoral issues. Local courts deal with issues regarding real estate records, family records, and banks.

The Supreme Court is the nation's highest court. The chief justice and twelve other justices decide cases. The chief justice is appointed by the president and approved of by the National Assembly. Other justices are appointed by the president, but they must be recommended by the chief justice. A chief justice holds office for six years and must retire at age seventy. The remaining justices also hold office for six years but must retire at age sixty-five. The justices hear appeals from lower courts to determine whether mistakes were made in trials at that level.

High courts hear civil, criminal, and administrative appeals of trials held in lower-level courts. District courts are located

Reporters capture a Supreme Court trial, broadcasting it live on television and the Internet.

A Strong Republic **67**

South Korea's National Government

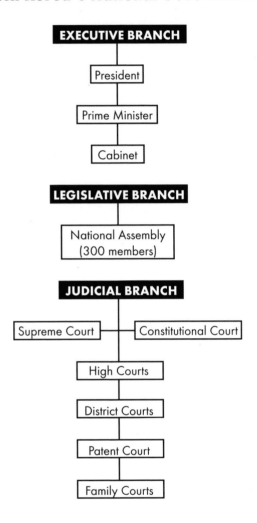

in thirteen major cities, and deal with both civil and criminal affairs. The patent court handles applications for protection of inventions. Family courts deal with issues such as marriage and divorce and crimes by young people. A special court called the Constitutional Court determines whether laws follow the constitution and handles disputes between different parts of government.

South Korea's Flag

The national flag of South Korea has three main parts: a white background, a red-and-blue symbol called the *taegeuk*, and four groups of black bars. The white background stands for peace. The taegeuk is the yin and yang symbol, which represents opposites that cannot exist without each other. When yin and yang are in balance, there is peace, happiness, and harmony. The black symbols, called *kwe*, stand for (clockwise from the upper left corner) heaven, water, earth, and fire.

Local Government

South Korea's constitution guarantees the rights of local governments to deal with all local matters of law, including property, marriages, and issues of local welfare. Local governments cannot pass laws that go against the constitution, but they can create local laws that deal with public properties, taxes, fees, and minor illegal acts.

Lower governments provide services depending on their districts. The three types of districts are *eup*, *myeon*, and *dong*. An eup is a division of a county or city with fewer than five hundred thousand residents. The minimum population for an eup is twenty thousand. A myeon is a township and is smaller than an eup. The minimum population of a myeon is six thousand people. A dong is the smallest or lowest level of administration and serves a small village. These divisions are administered by officials much like mayors. Every official has a council of advisers to assist in running the local government.

CHAPTER 6

On the Job

KIM TAE-YUN WORKS FOR THE MINISTRY OF Agriculture in Seoul monitoring the production rates of fruit and vegetable crops throughout South Korea. Kim's workday normally starts at 8:30 a.m., and lasts until 9:00 p.m. Although the official quitting time is 6:00 p.m., few employees dare leave then as it risks showing a lack of commitment to their jobs. Kim often works this schedule six days each week. Although South Korean law says that the workweek is five days and forty hours, one in five South Korean workers is on the job more than fifty-two hours a week.

When summer comes, Kim plans his annual vacation: a three-day trip to the mountains for hiking. According to law, employees who do not take any days off during the year should receive a paid, fifteen-day vacation every year, plus an extra day for every two years worked. However, few employees actually take their full time off.

Opposite: **Vendors and their customers at Seoul's Namdaemun Market, the largest traditional market in South Korea**

Kim's schedule is not unusual. South Koreans work longer hours on average than employees in any other industrialized country. They are known for a strong work ethic and a willingness to put in the time required to succeed.

South Korea's Agriculture

Traditionally, South Korea's economy was based on agriculture. Forty years ago, half of all workers were involved in farming, ranching, forestry, or fisheries. Today, that number has dropped to 6.6 percent of workers.

Some farmers grow bae, a kind of pear, which is also called Asian pear or apple pear.

The main crop in South Korea is rice. Nearly 80 percent of all farms grow it. Since rice is a staple in the South Korean diet, the government wants farmers to produce enough of it so that the country's demand is met. Farms also produce grains such as barley and wheat, along with soybeans, potatoes, cabbages, onions, and other fruits and vegetables.

South Koreans also raise livestock such as chickens, hogs, and cattle. Cattle farming is big business. Until the 1960s, cattle were used for plowing, but industrialization has changed that. Machines do the plowing and planting, and South Koreans look forward to beef on the dinner table. The favored breed is Hanwoo cattle, which provides 80 percent of beef products in South Korea.

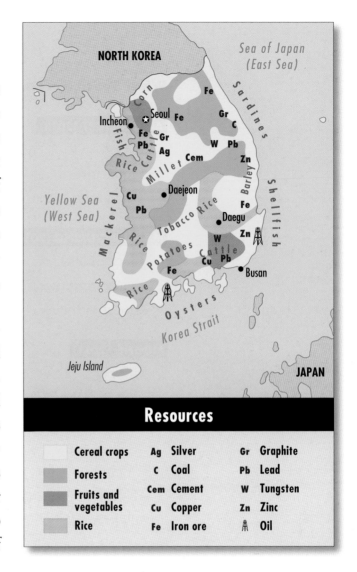

Although Koreans may prefer beef, they eat more pork because beef is more expensive. Chicken has never been popular, although fast-food and fried chicken restaurants are introducing more South Koreans to eating poultry.

South Korea has an active fishing industry that provides more than 3 million metric tons of fish yearly. Some of this comes from aquaculture, or fish farms. Major aquaculture prod-

What South Korea Grows, Makes, and Mines

AGRICULTURE (2013)

Rice	4,230,000 metric tons
Aquaculture	1,488,950 metric tons
Beef cattle	344,000 metric tons

MANUFACTURING (2012)

Electronics	US$107,800,000,000
Telecommunications equipment	US$17,976,000,000
Motor vehicles	4,657,000 vehicles

MINING (2011)

Copper	2,197,409 metric tons
Iron	542,000 metric tons
Feldspar	384,000 metric tons

ucts include oysters, clams, shrimp, and halibut. Throughout South Korea, fish and seafood are caught and shipped immediately to markets. Seoul, Busan, and several other cities have huge fresh fish markets that operate twenty-four hours a day.

Manufacturing

South Korea had little manufacturing history, but beginning in the 1960s, it expanded into an industrial giant, particularly in the fields of electronics, telecommunications, and automobile production. The growth in manufacturing in Seoul is called the Miracle on the Han River. During the 1970s and 1980s, Seoul primarily exported textiles and shoes. Since then, there

has been a huge growth in exports of automobiles, electronics, steel, and high-tech instruments, including computer monitors and cell phones.

During this period, many family-owned businesses, called *chaebols*, became international powerhouses. Along with massive growth came massive corruption and mismanagement. In 1997, a financial collapse caused the bankruptcy of the car company Daewoo, and the dismantling of a dozen of the large chaebols.

Employees assemble a car in a Hyundai factory. Hyundai is the largest automobile manufacturer in the country.

Chaebols

A *chaebol* is a South Korean corporation that is family owned and operated. Rather than small corner businesses, many chaebols are an economic force to be reckoned with. Large chaebols influence the government, gain government and bank loans easily, and employ large numbers of workers. South Korea's major chaebols include Samsung, Hyundai, LG, Hankook, and Daewoo.

Mining

South Korea's mining industry has enjoyed steady growth in recent years. Iron ore, feldspar, lead, zinc, and copper are among the primary minerals mined in South Korea. The country has a number of smelters that turn iron ore into steel. Graphite (a soft carbon mineral) and tungsten deposits are fairly large. South Korea also has an abundance of granite, marble, pyrophyllite, and talc.

Service Industries

The vast majority of South Korean workers, about 77 percent, are employed in service industries. These are industries in which people do things for others, rather than growing crops

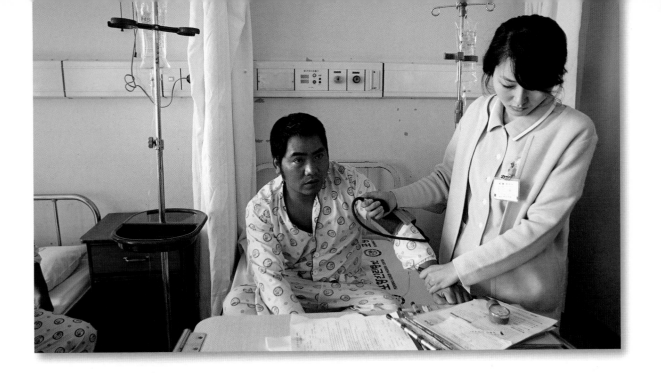

or manufacturing goods. People who work in service industries teach school, tend patients in hospitals, drive cabs, or handle money in banks. Major service sectors include banking, insurance, education, retail sales, and hospitality. Chefs, waiters, and hotel clerks are hospitality workers. Health care work is one of the fastest-growing sectors of service employment in South Korea. As the country ages, it needs more doctors, dentists, nurses, social workers, and caregivers.

More than two-thirds of South Korea's workers are in the service industry, many of them health care workers.

Transportation

South Korea is connected by air and sea to every other country. The country has eight major international airports, including modern facilities in Incheon, Seoul, and Busan. In South Korea, domestic flights take passengers to every city.

South Korea has a number of deep-water ports. Busan, the largest port, is located along Korea's southern coast and handles nearly 45 percent of the nation's shipping. Incheon Port serves as a gateway to Seoul, the capital city. Tonghae, on the east coast, handles the shipping of ore mines in the nearby mountains.

Most South Koreans who live in or near cities travel by rail or bus. High-speed rail lines connect the major cities, and buses run between and within cities. In cities, buses run regularly, and may be the cheapest way to get from one place to the next,

South Korea's high-speed trains provide fast, reliable transport across the country.

South Korea's currency is the won. Coins come in values of 10, 50, 100, and 500 won. Banknotes, or paper money, have values of 1,000, 5,000, 10,000, and 50,000 won. Each denomination has a different main color, a prominent Korean on the front, and an image related to that person on the back. For example, the blue 1,000-won note has a portrait of Confucian scholar Yi Hwang on the front and an image of a Confucian academy on the back. In 2014, 1,023 won equaled US$1.

short of walking or riding a bicycle. Seoul, Incheon, Busan, Daegu, and Daejeon have complex subway systems. Within Seoul, the basic fare for the subway is 1,050 won, or less than a dollar. Because so many cities are on the coast, ferries play an important role in transporting South Korean citizens.

Buying Power

Korean citizens work hard and long hours, but they enjoy a high standard of living, which is costly. In general, prices for standard items are 17 percent higher in Seoul than in the United States. Food prices tend to be 30 percent higher than in the United States, although South Koreans can sometimes save money at farmers' markets and open-air fish markets. Coffee is unusually expensive in South Korea. A cup of coffee in a café costs about US$6.

Housing costs about the same in South Korea as in the United States. Many people live in high-rise apartment buildings in cities. Living in the suburbs is much cheaper, but it adds to the cost of transportation, and it increases commuting time.

CHAPTER 7

A United People

JEONG AE-SOOK IS HAVING HER FIRST BIRTHDAY, called *doljanchi*. Family and friends are coming for the occasion. Her parents dress her in fancy clothing, which is based on traditional young women's gowns. A big part of the party is the *toljabee*, an event that is supposed to predict the direction the child's life will take. For this event, Ae-Sook is seated at a table covered with food and objects. The food includes rice, rice cakes, jujube, and fruits. The objects include pen and paper, a knife, money, books, needle and thread, a ruler, and a bow and arrow set.

Ae-Sook's parents encourage her to pick up one of these objects, which, according to Korean tradition, will link to the child's future. If Ae-Sook chooses a book or a pen and paper, for example, she will be a scholar. The choice of needle and thread means a long life, and the bow and arrow point

Opposite: **A child picks up a golf ball from the objects presented to her for the toljabee.**

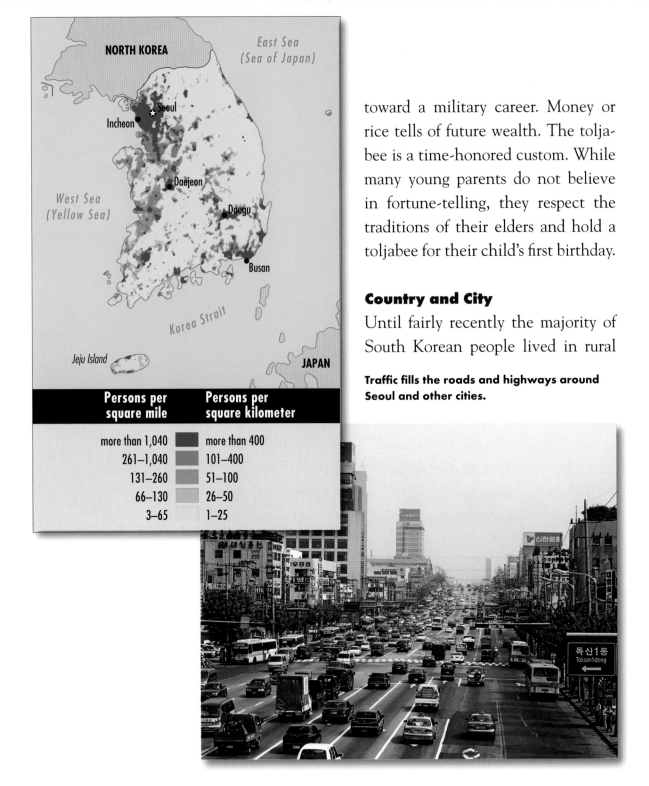

NORTH KOREA

*East Sea
(Sea of Japan)*

Seoul

Incheon

*West Sea
(Yellow Sea)*

Daejeon

Daegu

Busan

Korea Strait

Jeju Island

JAPAN

Persons per square mile	Persons per square kilometer
more than 1,040	more than 400
261–1,040	101–400
131–260	51–100
66–130	26–50
3–65	1–25

toward a military career. Money or rice tells of future wealth. The tolja-bee is a time-honored custom. While many young parents do not believe in fortune-telling, they respect the traditions of their elders and hold a toljabee for their child's first birthday.

Country and City

Until fairly recently the majority of South Korean people lived in rural

Traffic fills the roads and highways around Seoul and other cities.

There is an art to getting from one place to another in Seoul, and that art depends on knowing subway stops. Buildings on Seoul streets either are not numbered at all, or are numbered in a seemingly random order, according to when they were built. Thus, 142 X Street might stand between 2566 X Street and 5 X Street. This makes giving directions confusing. Seoul residents navigate by tall buildings and subway exits. Directions to taxi drivers work the same way. People tell a cabbie, "Let me off at the Hapjeong Station" or "It's two blocks away from Tower Palace One, Tower A."

areas, earning their living as farmers. Industrialization came late to South Korea, and, as a result, so did urban life. Seoul, a capital city for more than six hundred years, had as few as two hundred thousand residents only one hundred years ago. Between 1945 and 1985, Seoul's population grew from being 15 percent of the nation's total population to 65 percent. Within the next hundred years, it is expected that four out of five South Koreans will live in Seoul or its suburbs.

In 2014, South Korea had an estimated population of 49,039,986, and 83 percent of the people live in cities. The cities have become sprawling metropolitan areas, particularly in the northwest where Seoul, Incheon, Uijeongbu, Suwon, Hanam, and Ansan form a megalopolis. In Seoul, one of the most densely populated cities on earth, roughly 45,000 people live in every square mile (17,400 per square kilometer).

Most South Korean cities are on the coastlines, where sea transportation is available and inexpensive. The mountainous regions, particularly in the northeast, are sparsely populated. Many of these regions have a population density of less than a single person per square mile (1 per 2.6 sq km).

Chinatown in Incheon. In some South Korean cities, the resident Chinese population is large enough to support a community of China-focused shops, and restaurants.

Population of major cities (2013 est.)

Seoul	10,349,312
Busan	3,678,555
Incheon	2,628,000
Daegu	2,566,540
Daejeon	1,475,221

Who Lives in South Korea

The South Korean population is made up mostly of people born in Korea. The population has long been homogeneous, or similar, with only a small population of Chinese listed as permanent residents and an even smaller number of other minorities. In recent years, however, the number of immigrants has grown quickly, and many Koreans have begun to speak of the multiculturalism of South Korea. Many immigrants come from countries such as China, Vietnam, the Philippines, and Pakistan.

South Korea has one of the lowest birthrates in the world, with most families having only one child. Senior citizens, South Korea's fasting-growing age group, now make up 12 percent of the population. The life expectancy for Koreans is currently eighty years. This graying population is a concern to government officials, who see demands on health care, pensions, and senior facilities increasing.

The government has established policies that promote services for senior citizens. Seniors enjoy free travel on public transportation and free admission to parks and museums. Assisted-living housing is becoming more common. Once, the elderly lived with their families until they died, but as the population is becoming increasingly urban and housing is smaller, senior housing options have become a concern.

Ethnicity in South Korea (2012)

99.9% Korean

Experts estimate that seniors will make up about two-thirds of the South Korean population by 2050.

A person's sixtieth birthday is an important event in South Korea. In the lunar calendar there are sixty names for years. Every year of a person's life has a different name, but upon turning sixty, a person begins his or her "birth year" over, and the cycle begins again. This special birthday is called *hwangab*, and is accompanied by a feast. Some people celebrate their hwangab by taking trips with their family.

Going to School

Education is a priority for both parents and students in South Korea. Sometimes, half of a household's money goes toward educating its children. This education begins in nursery school. Parents are eager to get their children into quality day care that teaches reading, writing, math, and other subjects so the children will be well prepared when compulsory schooling begins at age six.

The South Korean school system is divided into three parts: six years of primary school, three years of middle school, and three years of high school. Most high schools are divided by gender, and even in coeducational high schools, classes tend to be all male or all female. Even though boys and girls are in separate classes, they learn the same material. All students must take both technology and home economics, which teaches skills useful at home.

Primary school covers many subjects: moral education, Korean language, social studies, math, science, physical education, music, fine arts, practical arts, and English. The goal is to produce well-educated, well-rounded citizens that support the community through hard work.

Students get used to schoolwork at an early age, which prepares them for the demands of middle school and beyond. Middle school consists of twelve subjects, electives, and extracurricular activities. Math, English, Korean language, social studies, and science have students grouped by ability. In ethics, arts, and physical education, students are not grouped by skills. Foreign languages and environmental education are possible electives.

Many South Korean middle and high school students study foreign languages such as English, Japanese, Chinese, German, French, or Spanish.

The core curriculum of high schools is similar to the requirements in the United States or Canada. There are several levels of science offered, as well as history, political science, economics, and cultural studies. The Ministry of Education also offers vocational high schools, where those interested in vocational skills, such as automotive maintenance, cooking, and technology repair, get specific training in their chosen fields.

Classes in South Korean high schools can be large, and it is not unusual to find fifty students in one class. Still, discipline is not an issue, as students are taught from an early age to respect teachers and act accordingly.

Getting into college is highly competitive. In addition to going to school until 5:00 p.m. each day, high school students hoping to get into college go to "cram schools," called *hagwon*.

Beautiful cherry trees blossom on the campus of Kyung Hee University in Seoul.

Cram schools are private academies that provide supplementary education for students. They also help students who may have fallen behind due to illness; train students in areas not covered by regular high schools; and help those who want to improve college-testing scores. About 69 percent of males and 74 percent of females graduating from high school go on to college or university.

The Korean Language

Korean is the primary language of both South and North Korea. Korea's close historic links to China are seen in the influence the Chinese language has on the Korean national language. About 50 percent of Korean words and characters come directly from Chinese. The Korean alphabet is called hangul. As in the Latin alphabet used for English, each symbol stands for a vowel or consonant sound. In Korean, there are ten vowels and fourteen consonants.

CHAPTER 8

Matters of Faith

THE ALARM GOES OFF AT 6:15 A.M., AND PARK SU-MIN rises. Instead of scurrying around, chasing children, and serving breakfast, Park eases herself to the floor and folds her legs into the lotus position. Breathing deeply, she begins fifteen minutes of meditation. She clears her mind and reviews the Four Essentials of Won Buddhism: developing self-power, learning the primary role of wisdom, educating others' children, and honoring public-spirited citizens.

The third essential is easy for Park. She teaches mathematics at the local technology high school. The other three do not come so quickly. Park's days are long, with classes, preparation, meetings, and after-school tutoring. However, a follower of Won Buddhism accepts the long days and the demands of her job as part of her life. For Won Buddhists, all life is in the Buddha, and the Buddha is in all life.

Opposite: **Buddhists pray during a ceremony celebrating the Buddha's birthday.**

Religion in South Korea

Religion in South Korea	
Buddhist	24%
Protestant	19%
Catholic	11%
Other	2%
No religion	43%

Seoul's Yoido Full Gospel Church has the largest number of members of any Pentecostal church in the world. Pentecostalism is a branch of Christianity.

Religion in South Korea

For centuries, Korea's rulers dictated which religion their people would follow. Kings and emperors who favored Buddhism insisted that their subjects follow Buddhism. Those leaders who followed Confucian doctrine imposed it on Korean citizens.

Today, religion is in a state of flux in South Korea. There is no state religion, and there is no dominant religion, but Christianity is becoming increasingly prominent in many aspects of social and political life. Today, about 19 percent of the population is Protestant. Another 11 percent is Catholic. Twenty-four percent identify as Buddhist, while about 2 percent follow other religions. The greatest percentage—some 43 percent—claim to follow no religion at all.

Shamanism

A shaman is a person who acts as a link between the everyday world and the supernatural. Shamans may heal people, tell the future, control angry spiritual forces, or determine when gods favor a certain activity. Shamanism, a form of folk religion, has been practiced in Korea since early times when shamans led prayers and sacrifices for plentiful rainfall and good harvests. They prayed over the sick to heal them and the dying to ease the passage into the next world.

While Shamanism flourished during the Silla, Paekche, and Koguryo kingdoms, it was oppressed during the Joseon dynasty, when Confucianism was the state religion. When Korea was a Japanese colony, shamanism was forbidden. In modern South Korea, some people still rely on shamanism. Many Koreans visit a *jeomjip* (fortune-teller's shop) or *saju* café (fortune-teller café) before making a major life decision, such

A shaman performs a ceremony for the people who died in a ferry accident in 2014.

as moving, marrying, or having children. Some fortune-tellers are highly respected, and having one's fortune determined is a popular trend in South Korea.

Confucianism

The philosopher Confucius developed a moral code for living, and Confucianism is less a religion than an ethical, philosophical life plan. Confucianism is based on specific ideals: generosity, love of others, righteous behavior, dignity, and wisdom. By pursuing these ideals, followers of Confucius established suitable management of both family and public life.

In Korea in the fourth century, students of Confucius studied in universities and then taught in provincial academies. By the tenth century, Confucianism and Buddhism survived side by side. It was possible to follow Buddhism as a religion and study Confucius's teachings for the discipline and integrity needed for daily living. In 1392, the Joseon ruler established Confucianism as the official principles that guided education, royal ceremonies, and government policy. Confucian followers openly opposed Japanese rule during the 1900s, and Japan crushed Confucianism as it did any opposing beliefs.

Today, there are few followers of Confucianism in South Korea, but the basic concepts of honoring one's ancestors and revering one's parents are cornerstones of Korean life. According to Confucian belief, proper social order can be secured by maintaining five major relationships in life, and Koreans cherish these steadfastly throughout their lives. The relationships are those between friends, between old and

young, between husband and wife, between father and son, and between king (or employer) and minister (employee).

A monk prays in the Tongdosa temple in southern South Korea. One of the largest Buddhist temples in Asia, it was built in the 600s.

Buddhism

Buddhism is equal parts religion and philosophy. Buddhists follow the teachings of a man named Siddhartha Gautama. He was a teacher and philosopher who lived in India sometime between the sixth and fourth centuries BCE. Gautama spent his life trying to gain an understanding of why suffering exists, and to learn how to move past suffering to live in harmony. As his teachings spread, he became known as the Buddha, or enlightened one.

Buddhism was introduced to Korea in 372 CE by a monk visiting the Koguryo kingdom. In 384, a monk named Malananda introduced Buddhism to Paekche. Ado, a monk

Manggyeongsa Temple

South Korea has about twenty thousand Buddhist temples. One of the most stunning is Manggyeongsa Temple, which is located high in the Taebaek Mountains. According to legend, a stone statue of the Buddha sitting cross-legged on a lotus blossom drew the attention of a monk during the Silla period. The monk built the temple to honor the Buddha. Near the temple, there is a hot-water spring called the Dragon Spring. High in the mountains, the spring steams amid snow-covered pines.

who lived during the fifth century, traveled to Silla, and taught the ways of Buddhist enlightenment there. By the time of Unified Silla, Buddhism had taken hold, and people continued to follow the teachings of Buddha through the Joseon dynasty. In the 1900s, the Japanese tried to get Korean Buddhists to practice in the same way as Japanese Buddhists, but they were unsuccessful.

Buddhists follow the Four Noble Truths that make up the basic ideas of Buddha's teachings: the truth of suffering, the cause of suffering, the end of suffering, and the path to end suffering. The goal of Buddhists is to reach nirvana, or enlightenment, through an endless cycle of rebirth.

Won Buddhism is a form of Buddhism that has been molded to fit modern South Korea. The teachings of the Buddha have been simplified so that the path to enlightenment is clear to everyone. In many ways, Won Buddhism is an easier religion to follow than traditional Buddhism. While traditional Buddhism requires that followers forgo material wealth, Won Buddhism states that wealth is not an issue. Won Buddhism accepts that differences in wealth, work, and external living conditions do not bar followers from reaching nirvana.

Won Buddhists do not pray in monasteries, but practice their religion in the everyday world: at work, with friends, in the community, and among family. It is up to followers of Won Buddhism to live a good and honest life, protect the helpless, honor others, and always be just in their dealings.

Catholicism

Catholicism was introduced into Korea in the 1600s when information about Western learning first came to Korea with

Pope Francis, the head of the Roman Catholic Church, greets a nun after arriving in South Korea for a visit in 2014.

A Cathedral in Seoul

Myeong-dong Cathedral, built between 1894 and 1898, is the primary Catholic church in Korea. A huge building, the cathedral features a 148-foot (45 m) brick tower as its focal point. Inside, graceful pillars support tall arches and frame the church's many stained-glass windows. In the basement, a small burial site protects the remains of Catholic people killed when the government tried to rid Korea of Catholicism. Bronze doors feature a frieze of the conversion of Koreans to Catholicism.

scholars from China. The first Catholic priest to arrive was Chinese priest Zhou Wen-mo in 1794.

More Koreans have been turning to the Catholic Church. According to some reports, the number of Catholics in Korea has increased by 2 to 3 percent per year in recent years. More than half of all Korean Catholics live in Seoul, Suwon, Incheon, and Uijeongbu.

Protestantism

A Presbyterian named Horace Allen was the first Protestant missionary in Korea. He arrived in 1884. The following year, a Methodist Episcopal missionary came, and the door to Protestant Christianity was open. Many missionaries made inroads into Korean society by providing medical services and opening schools.

Protestant churches promoted Christian ideals, supporting Christian schools and social reform. They spoke out in

Religious Holidays

New Year	1st full moon in January
Buddha's Birthday	1st full moon in May
Christmas	December 25

Cheondogyo is centered in Seoul, where the Cheondogyo Central Temple was built between 1918 and 1921.

favor of nationalism and equality between males and females. They also tried to promote political and religious freedom.

Cheondogyo

Cheondogyo, the Religion of the Heavenly Way, is a native Korean religion. The primary concept is to dedicate oneself to bringing peace and fairness into the world. Cheondogyo followers honor God by placing clean water on ritual altars. They meditate about God, offer prayers, and avoid sinful thoughts. The followers believe in *innaecheon*, the concept that man and God are one.

Cheondogyo was established by a Korean named Choe Je-u in 1860. By the end of the 1900s, there were three million Cheondogyo followers.

CHAPTER 9

National Treasures, Everyday Pleasures

NO YU-SANG IS A SOUTH KOREAN NATIONAL treasure. He is a master kite maker. During the year, No, called "Mr. Kite," visits hundreds of primary schools, teaching children how to make kites and demonstrating kite flying and the tactics of kite fighting. Every year, he looks forward to the lunar New Year, when the annual kite-fighting contest is held in Seoul. In 2014, more than sixty of the contestants had been introduced to the art of kite flying and kite fighting by No.

The contestants make their own kites and embed broken ceramics in the lines to create sharp edges. When fighting, they use their abrasive lines to cut the kite strings of their opponents, thereby winning the competition. Kite fighting is not a sport for children. The flyers are more likely to be lawyers, teachers, or officers in the military.

Kite flying is a long Korean tradition, dating back to 637 CE. During the reign of Queen Chindok, who ruled from 647 to 654, General Kim Yu-sin flew a kite over the night sky of

Opposite: **Many kite festivals are held in South Korea every year.**

A practitioner of tae kwon do breaks a board with a kick during a show in Seoul.

Gyeongju. He had a flaming cotton ball hanging from the kite, which onlookers thought was a shooting star. The renowned Admiral Yi also used kites. In the sixteenth century, Yi signaled his troops with kites as the Japanese invaded.

Sports of All Sorts

Koreans have long had an interest in sports and games, but that interest became fanatical when Seoul hosted the Summer Olympic Games in 1988. In preparation for the games, South Korea built a number of world-class facilities in Seoul and its suburbs. A new outdoor stadium, gymnasiums for basketball, a boxing arena, an indoor swimming pool, and a baseball stadium improved the opportunities for athletics through the Seoul area. After the Olympics ended, the new arenas expanded to give young Koreans training facilities, a skating rink for speed skating and figure skating, and venues for fencing, weight lifting, and tennis.

Koreans pursue a number of sports, both as athletes and spectators. One sport growing in popularity is golf. Several South Koreans are professional golfers, and Koreans flock to golf courses. When the weather is too chilly for golf, young people head to ski resorts in Gangwon and Gyeonggi provinces.

When the weather is clear, Koreans take to the outdoors. National parks and preserves have hiking trails through mountains, wetlands, and coastal areas. Mountain climbing and rock climbing have a growing following, as do hunting and fishing. Vacationers to Jeju often fish from the shore or hire deep-sea fishing boats for a day on the ocean.

Martial arts provide excellent exercise, and academies for tae kwon do teach students of all ages how to control their bodies, minds, and spirits through discipline and practice. Slightly less popular is the practice of gong kwon yusul. It is a combination of various martial art forms, with techniques taken from hapkido, jujitsu, and judo. Competitors learn to

Golfing Great

Inbee Park is a professional golfer with nine tour victories. She was the 2013 Rolex Player of the Year and the 2012 tour money winner. Born in Seoul, South Korea, in 1988, Park began playing golf at age ten. She attended Kwangwoon University and became a professional in 2006. With four major wins already, Park may well become South Korea's greatest woman golfer.

National Treasures, Everyday Pleasures **103**

Ssireum

A traditional Korean wrestling sport, ssireum is most common as a folk competition. Two players hold on to a *satba*, a red sash tied to the waist and thigh. The two struggle until one falls to the ground. Ssireum originated during the time when people wrestled beasts for food, but it eventually became a tournament at which the winner earned a bull as the reward for victory. Today, South Korea has professional ssireum teams.

strike, throw, and control opponents through swift moves, footwork, and some boxing-style actions. Ssireum is another martial art that is more like wrestling.

Team sports begin at a young age for South Koreans. Most large cities have baseball and soccer teams. There are also youth leagues, such as Little League for baseball and school competitions in soccer, basketball, and cycling. Baseball is even more popular in Korea than in Japan. Families head to the stadiums to cheer on their local teams. In the fall, the championship Korean Series has families glued to television sets, anxious to see if a favorite team wins. In 2014, South Korea won the Little League World Series Championship for the first time since 1985.

Local parks are usually equipped with basketball courts, tennis courts, and shallow swimming pools. Parks also have soccer fields, and there are teams at all levels from children's leagues through professionals. In 2002, South Korea and Japan cohosted the World Cup, the world's biggest soccer tournament, and this event increased interest in the sport.

Cycling has been both a mode of transportation and a form of recreation. Bike lanes on main streets and in parks provide safe biking trails. Mountain biking has an increasing following, and many Koreans head to the mountains with their bikes hooked on the back of their cars.

Games

Winters in South Korea are long and cold. Traditional games have kept Koreans entertained through the long nights. Among the most popular games are *baduk*, *hwatu*, *janggi*, and *yut nori*. Baduk is a strategic game, played with black and white button-shaped markers and a grid. The idea is for one player to block off more territory than the opponent by enclosing and capturing the opponent's markers with his or her own markers.

Hwatu is a deck of cards used for playing several different games. The hwatu are flower cards with pictures to represent each month. The cards are laid out in a circle. Each player starts with ten cards, and players take turns picking and discarding cards. The object is to match the cards in one's hand, and many people gamble on the outcome of each match.

Janggi is the Korean version of chess, and it is common to find men crouched over janggi boards throughout public parks. Janggi pieces are slightly different from those in classic chess. In janggi the pieces for each player consist of one general, two chariots, two cannons, two horses, two elephants, two guards, and five soldiers. The object of the game is to capture the general.

Yut nori (yut play) is a board game played during the Korean New Year. Dating back to the Three Kingdoms period, yut nori requires a board, markers, and yut sticks. Players toss the sticks

Pieces in a janggi set are traditionally red and green.

and move according to the order in which the sticks fall. The plan is to get one's markers "home" before the opponent can.

Outdoors children play a game called *jegichagi*, which is a kicking game, like hacky sack. The children kick a *jegi*, which is made of a coin and paper, and try to keep it in the air. The jegi can be passed from one player to another, or from one foot to the other. The game can also be played with a group in a circle, passing the jegi around from child to child.

Music and Dance

Years ago, Korean music and dance were linked to either the court or folk traditions. The National Center for Korean Traditional Performing Arts has brought back these arts, most of which were once banned by the Japanese. The center, located in Seoul, employs both artists and researchers in an effort to preserve classical Korean court music and folk traditions.

Traditional Korean musical instruments are divided into categories based on the materials that produce the sounds. There are eight sounds, made by skin, silk, bamboo, metal, earth, stone, gourds, and wood. Skin instruments include small handheld drums and large kettle-style drums. The *gayageum*, a twelve-stringed zither, is a silk instrument, while bamboo instruments include flutes that buzz and flutes that whistle.

Traditional court music is slow, and the emphasis is on specific tones rather than a melody. Court music depends on a five-note scale, with little or no harmony.

Historically, some court dances were performed only for royalty, and not seen by ordinary citizens until the twentieth century.

The gayageum is considered the national instrument of South Korea.

Hwagwanmu, the flower crane dance, has been resurrected by the center and performed for the public, along with *Cheoyongmu*, a masked dance based on the legend of the Dragon King.

Pansori is a form of storytelling in song. The songs are presented with one singer and a drummer. The songs are hundreds of years old. Many pansori date from the seventeenth century.

Changgeuk, traditional Korean opera, features twenty to thirty performers and an orchestra. The content is usually full of humor and social satire. Many stories in changgeuk have one character that is clever and one that is easily tricked, and a host of classic characters such as heroes, villains, and fools.

The National Dance Company thrives by presenting traditional dance, folk dance, and modern Korean dance. The costumes are vivid, and the dances present classic themes of Korean literature. *The Scent of Ink* and *Altar* are two presentations that are cutting-edge and contemporary in style, while representing Korean philosophy. *The Scent of Ink* consists of scenes based on classic floral symbols—plum blossom, orchid, chrysanthemum, and bamboo—evoking for audiences writing paper and ink-and-wash painting. *Altar* mixes the ancient music of shamans with the opera of German composer Richard Wagner. The dance addresses the altar as a symbol of romance, religion, and social awareness.

South Korea has its own version of pop music, called K-pop, that features synthesized music and complex dance routines. K-pop mixes pop music with disco, rock, R&B, and hip-hop. Bands feature well-trained singers and exciting cho-

Dancers perform a traditional Korean dance.

Gangnam Style

K-pop hit the United States with a bang when South Korean musician Psy introduced "Gangnam Style." Recorded in 2011, "Gangnam Style" became a singing and dancing phenomenon. More than two billion people have viewed the music video on the Internet. The song refers to the Gangnam District of Seoul. "Gangnam Style" topped the charts in thirty countries around the world. World leaders, including President Barack Obama and British prime minister David Cameron, mimicked the dance without success. No one could match the style of Psy!

reography. Up-and-coming stars sometimes sign with agencies at the age of nine or ten. They go into training to learn how to sing, play instruments, speak several languages, and dance, which over the years can cost an agency more than US$3 million. The popular nine-member band, Girls' Generation, formed by such an agency, is currently the top paid group.

Visual Arts

South Korea's artistic history dates back centuries and blends many influences. Much of the surviving art from the Three Kingdoms period was found in tombs. These artworks include murals of daily life, hunting scenes and weapons, jewelry, and bronze work. Because this period was a time when Buddhism became popular, many statues of Buddha, carved from stone or worked in bronze or gold, have survived. During the Unified Silla period that followed, Buddhist temples were built, and artwork to adorn these temples was produced.

During the Koryo dynasty, China exerted a strong influence on all aspects of Korean art. Korean nobles wanted Chinese-style artwork. The fine art of Korean calligraphy was modeled after Chinese works, as were literature, poetry, and music. Architects designed complex temples. The walls, ceilings, and floors of these temples were covered in lacquer, making them hard and shiny, and inlaid with beautiful mother-of-pearl seashells. The temples featured many golden statues and watercolors of Buddhist scenes.

The Joseon period saw subtle changes in art. Landscape painting, ceramics, and religious art dominated. Landscapes were painted in the An Gyeon style, named for an artist popular at the start of the Joseon period. Typically this style featured cloud-covered mountains and dense pine trees.

An interesting aspect of Joseon art is that a number of artists came from the royal family. Yi Am and Yi Jeong were grandsons of King Sejong, while Yi Gyeong-yun was a great-

Korean Folk Painting

Korean folk painting relies on the use of traditional symbols. This unique art form was created for common citizens to keep in their homes. The art represents specific aspects of life: luck, long life, and security. The turtle, dragon, and unicorn symbolize good luck. The deer, crane, clouds, water, bamboo, and pine represent long life. Guardians to watch over the family include the tiger at the front door or a dragon at the gate. These traditional symbols were passed down from one generation to the next and are still used in artworks today.

A woman looks at
a painting by Kim
Ki-Chang. Kim was a
master modern artist.

grandson of King Seongjong. Joseon artists often depicted meetings between important government officials. These paintings were usually made as keepsakes after a visit to court.

Modern Korean art began with the end of Japanese occupation in 1945. The postwar period saw a major change from traditional Japanese-influenced art forms to art that was radical, modern, and colorful. Artists such as Kim Ki-Chang, Pak Nae-hyon, and Pak No-su had classical training, which they put to use in producing bold, abstract art created with ink, watercolors, and acrylic paints.

Animation and Movies

Modern art in Korea has taken a turn toward cartooning and animation. In the 1970s and 1980s, many Japanese animation studios developed Korea's cartooning expertise by using Koreans to do the labor-intensive coloring. There are about

120 animation studios in the Seoul area, and they turn out massive amounts of work that is seen worldwide. Much of *The Simpsons*, *Family Guy*, *Phineas and Ferb*, and *The Legend of Korra* has been drawn and produced in Seoul. There are also artists who draw *manhwa*, the Korean version of Japanese *manga*, and Western graphic novels.

The South Korean movie industry has rapidly evolved into a world player. Blockbuster movies from Korean studios include *Shiri* (1999), *JSA* (2000), and *Chingu* (2001). Korean movies range from romantic comedies to science fiction to organized crime thrillers.

The most fascinating thing about Korean movies is the theaters themselves. In addition to regular theaters, audiences can choose 3-D and 4-D theaters. In a 4-D theater, viewers see, hear, and experience the events of the movie complete with shaking seats, water spray, and puffs of air. South Korea also has "lounge" theaters, where the viewers sit in recliners and can order gourmet dinners while they watch the movie.

CHAPTER 10

Family First

YI JI-HAE IS ONE HUNDRED DAYS OLD, WHICH IN South Korea is cause for celebration. It was not too long ago that many infants died before reaching this very young age. Ji-hae's parents are modern Koreans, but they will follow the custom of celebrating this milestone because their parents wish it.

The family eats soup and rice to honor the grandmother spirit that has watched over Ji-hae. Relatives come and celebrate with rice cakes, wine, and sweet red and black bean cakes. To make sure Ji-hae will have good luck, red bean cakes are put at the four compass points in the house. For Ji-hae's long life, the family shares rice cakes with as many as one hundred people. The house is filled with visitors, but, like most young babies, Ji-hae sleeps through the entire event.

Opposite: **South Korean mothers traditionally carry their young babies in a sling on their back.**

National Holidays

New Year's Day	January 1
Lunar New Year's Day	1st day of the first lunar month
Independence Movement Day	March 1
Children's Day	May 5
Buddha's Birthday	8th day of the fourth lunar month
Memorial Day	June 6
Constitution Day	July 17
Liberation Day	August 15
Harvest Moon Festival (*Chuseok*)	15th day of the eighth lunar month
Foundation Day	October 3
Hangul Day	October 9
Christmas Day	December 25
New Year's	December 31–January 2

Celebrating Together

South Koreans celebrate some of the same holidays that people in other countries celebrate. For example, Christmas and New Year's are national holidays. Other holidays are unique to South Korea.

In 1923, children's book writer Bang Jeong-hwan introduced a new holiday concept to Korea: Children's Day. Bang said, "Children are the heroes of tomorrow. May they grow to be gentle, vigorous, and wise." Today, Children's Day is a national holiday. To celebrate, parents give their children gifts and spend the day doing something fun for the entire family, such as going to a zoo or amusement park, or seeing a movie. In Seoul's Children's Grand Park, children ride on ponies or camels, slip and slide at the Water Playground, or scream and thrill on the roller coaster.

In rural Korea, festivals parallel the farm calendar. The first day of the lunar New Year is celebrated with feasts and dancing. On Dano, the fifth day of the fifth lunar month, farmers gather to celebrate the end of sowing seeds for spring and summer harvests.

Chuseok, the autumn harvest festival, is a time for families to return to their roots. Families gather to enjoy feasts and visit ancestral graves. At family graves, the young bow in respect and clear the area of weeds. Family members offer gifts, such as fruit or meat. Upon returning to the family home, they

Some people cannot visit their ancestral hometowns for Chuseok because those towns lie across the border in North Korea. Instead, they celebrate near the DMZ.

Traditional Korean Clothing

The traditional clothing of South Korea is a set of silk robes called the *hanbok*. Traditional robes are usually worn only for weddings and on New Year's and Chuseok. Like many other traditions, wearing hanbok is fading from practice.

light candles and set the table, with each dish in a specific location. It is an honored custom to share Chuseok foods with those who are unable to return to the ancestral family village.

The Value of Family

Korean children grow up in a family-oriented environment. As the children grow, families emphasize respect for one's parents and grandparents. This includes taking care of them in their old age, mourning their loss when they die, and honoring their traditions. Children are raised believing they owe a debt to their parents and grandparents, and part of that debt is continuing family lines. As part of the New Year's ritual, the younger generation dresses in traditional hanbok and bows to honor their grandparents.

Good Manners

In many ways, young people in South Korea are much like young people in the United States and Canada. In both places, it is common to see teenagers wearing jeans and T-shirts and texting on their phones. Although South Korean teens and children enjoy Western video games and music, traditional Korean manners are still expected. Appropriate behavior is a critical factor in daily Korean life.

Koreans believe in the concept of face. Face is the outward, social status of a person, and losing face is considered a form of public humiliation. It is never acceptable for children or teens to be rude to adults, ignore adults, or show disrespect in any way. For example, young travelers immediately offer their bus seats to the elderly, pregnant women, or women with children.

Eating customs in South Korea vary from those in some other parts of the world. It is fine to slurp soup in a restaurant, but it is not acceptable to stick chopsticks upright in a bowl of rice. That would look too much like the incense burners used at funerals. Every meal has rice, and most have kimchee, a fermented cabbage dish. Visitors are expected to eat what is served. It is poor etiquette to make negative comments about the food.

Two teenagers pose for a picture with a ceremonial guard at Gyeongbokgung Palace in Seoul.

Warmth from Below

Ondol (warm stone) is a heated floor, and most Korean homes have one. The heat is passed in pipes under the floor. Because winters are so cold, most Koreans sit on the heated floor. This system of heating goes back to the Koguryo dynasty (37 BCE–668 CE). In South Korea, more than 90 percent of houses have ondol or radiant floor heating. People eat, watch TV, and sleep on the floor.

South Koreans also remove their shoes when they visit other people's houses. Wearing shoes inside is viewed as highly disrespectful.

Marriage

One hundred years ago, young Korean men and women married the spouses chosen by their parents. A matchmaker scouted potential brides and selected appropriate matches. The bride was expected to be quiet and accepting of whatever decision her parents made. The groom knew his duty was to marry the chosen bride—often a woman he would meet for the first time at the wedding—and produce children. Fifty years ago, young men were given a list of potential brides, interviewed them, and selected one.

Courting rituals have changed since then. Young men and women date whom they choose, and they select their own spouses. However, there are still customs to be observed. A groom asks potential in-laws for their permission to marry their daughter. Even if the bride has an engagement ring, the engagement is not official without the parents' approval.

Parents pay for the wedding, with costs divided between the two families. The bride's family pays for half of the wedding expenses, half the honeymoon, all furniture for the married couple's home, and a wedding gift for the groom's family. In addition to paying for the other half of the wedding and honeymoon, the groom's family pays the cost of the apartment for the new couple, and also for a gift for the bride's family.

The wedding service is a two-part event. There is a Western-style ceremony, with the bride wearing a white dress and the groom a tuxedo, and a traditional event with the couple dressed in hanbok. The two weddings honor both the world of young Koreans and the customs of their ancestors.

Young married couple

Traditional Wedding Clothing

Grooms wear an overcoat, called a *durumagi*, which is usually purple silk. The durumagi goes over the jacket and loose-fitting pants. Grooms also wear *kkotsin*, silk shoes with embroidered flowers, and a *gat*, a wide-brimmed black hat.

Brides wear a *jeogori*, a short, white, decorated top. The *dongjeong* is a white collar worn at the neckline around the jeogori. *Otgoreum* are cloth strings that hang over the *chima* (skirt) of the gown. A chima is an outer skirt, which can be several layers or quilted. *Beoseon*, or socks, finish off the outfit.

Good to Eat

Rice is the main staple of the Korean diet. People eat wheat in breads, noodles, and cakes, but rice is eaten three times a day. Another staple is kimchee, which is spicy, pickled, seasoned cabbage. Kimchee is so vital to Korean meals that people hold festivals for making it. In the past, when the cabbage harvest came in, women made enough kimchee to last a winter. Cabbage and white radish were cut, washed, and salted. The ingredients were packed in earthenware jars, which were sealed and buried in the backyard. When food was sparse, women dug up the jar, added red pepper, garlic, or other vegetables, and then cooked the kimchee to make a meal. This

Rice and kimchee are a basic part of every meal.

vegetable dish is so prized by Koreans that many apartment dwellers buy small electric kimchee coolers for their homes.

Koreans use a wide range of vegetables, spices, and herbs in their cooking. Spinach, lettuce, mung beans, and soybeans can be grown in a household garden or purchased at the local market. Pepper, salt, soy sauce, garlic, and onions are common seasonings. Among the lesser-known ingredients found in Korean pantries are wild aster, marsh plant, daylily, bellflower, and royal fern bracken. Many of these ingredients can be picked in the wild, as they are common wildflowers.

Koreans eat soup often. A popular soup is *dongtae jjigae*, a chowder made with fresh pollock, bell peppers, onions, radishes, hot peppers, tofu, and mushrooms. This dish is often served during winter months and is hot in both temperature and spiciness. Oxtail soup, on the other hand, is flavored only with salt and onions.

Street foods fill cities with marvelous aromas. *Ddukbokki* are cylinder-shaped rice cakes cooked in a spicy red sauce. Every street vendor has a special recipe, adding fish cakes, vegetables, or boiled eggs to the mix. *Hotteok*, hot pancakes, sizzle on street grills and can have a tasty filling of brown sugar, cinnamon, and walnuts. *Yangnyeom tongtak*, Korean-style fried chicken, really is finger-licking good. Each piece is triple-cooked in batter and coated with a spicy red sauce. *Bibimbap* is a classic Korean dish. It includes vegetables, rice, and an egg, but the specific ingredients can vary tremendously.

School lunch in South Korea is nothing like lunch in U.S. schools. A Korean student is served some form of soup, rice,

Vegetable Bibimbap

Every chef makes bibimbap a little differently. Have an adult help you make this version.

Ingredients

2 tablespoons oil

1 cup carrots, cut in matchsticks

1 cup zucchini, cut in matchsticks

½ cup bean sprouts, fresh

6 ounces bamboo shoots, canned, drained

4.5 ounces mushrooms, canned, drained

2 cups white rice, cooked

⅓ cup green onions, sliced thin

2 tablespoons soy sauce

¼ teaspoon black pepper, ground

1 tablespoon butter

4 eggs

4 teaspoons red chili sauce

Directions

1. In a large skillet, heat the oil and cook the carrots and zucchini until soft, about 5 minutes.
2. Add the bean sprouts, bamboo shoots, and mushrooms and cook the mixture another 3 minutes, stirring to turn the vegetables. Add the rice and heat through.
3. Add the green onions, soy sauce, and pepper. Cover and put aside.
4. Warm a medium skillet and add butter. Fry the eggs.
5. Divide the vegetable and rice mixture into four soup bowls. Cover each amount of vegetable and rice mixture with a fried egg. Top each with a teaspoon of red chili sauce. Dig in!

two or three side dishes, and some form of protein. A typical menu for one school day might be rice, kimchee stew, radish kimchee, cucumber kimchee, and boneless fried chicken. Another day lunch might be rice; soybean paste soup with potatoes, mushrooms, and pumpkin; coleslaw; cabbage kimchee; and bulgogi (barbecued) beef.

Student lunches have the same basic elements as any other meal, including rice, kimchee, and soup.

Funeral Traditions

For most nations, death rites follow the family's religious beliefs. In South Korea, people follow whichever rites they choose, but most families select Confucian customs. Traditionally, Koreans believed that if a person died away from home, that person's spirit would wander endlessly. To prevent such an event, families tried to bring even the sickest relatives home before they died.

Customarily, when death was only moments away, family members wailed their sorrow. The family changed into mourning clothes. The women put aside their jewelry, and the family stopped combing their hair. A family member took the deceased person's coat and stood on the roof. From there, the deceased's name was called out three times so that all neighbors could hear. The day after the death, the body was washed with perfumed water. After being bathed and dressed in traditional funeral dress, the body was wrapped in quilted cloth.

The coffin was carried to the gravesite on a large wooden frame lashed together with straw rope. This frame was often brightly decorated. At the funeral, as the coffin was lowered into the grave, the oldest son bowed and tossed dirt upon the coffin. Often, a memorial service followed.

While many families still follow this tradition, more people are choosing cremation as an alternative to traditional burial rites. In the past, cremation was believed to dishonor the deceased. Today, nearly 75 percent of the dead are cremated. Land is at a premium, and funeral plots are very expensive. Many people are opting for natural burials, placing cremated remains

In a traditional burial, family members and friends help carry the body to the burial site.

in the soil around trees. Markers on the trees identify those who have passed on. Other South Koreans are having their relatives' ashes turned into beads. Burial beads come in blue-green, pink, or black. They can be placed in a glass container and displayed in the home. The process costs about US$900.

Though the culture is changing, South Koreans continue to practice their ancestors' traditions while embracing modern life. Many people have moved to cities in recent decades, making South Korea a less rural nation than it was in the past; the traditional family structure with only the father going to work is giving way to two-income families; and students spend more time at school than at home; yet through it all, from birth to death, family remains central to the South Korean way of life.

Timeline

SOUTH KOREAN HISTORY

Humans settle in what is now Korea. **ca. 30,000 BCE**

The Three Kingdoms arise in Korea. **1st century BCE**

The Unified Silla dynasty gains control of Korea. **668 CE**

The Kingdom of Koryo gains power. **935**

Yi Song-gye founds the Joseon dynasty. **1392**

Admiral Yi Sun-sin uses ironclad turtle ships to defeat the Japanese. **1598**

Catholicism arrives in Korea. **1783**

Korea opens three ports to international trade. **1876**

The Donghak Uprising leads to the Sino-Japanese War for control of Korea. **1894**

Queen Min is murdered. **1895**

WORLD HISTORY

ca. 2500 BCE The Egyptians build the pyramids and the Sphinx in Giza.

ca. 563 BCE The Buddha is born in India.

313 CE The Roman emperor Constantine legalizes Christianity.

610 The Prophet Muhammad begins preaching a new religion called Islam.

1054 The Eastern (Orthodox) and Western (Roman Catholic) Churches break apart.

1095 The Crusades begin.

1215 King John seals the Magna Carta.

1300s The Renaissance begins in Italy.

1347 The plague sweeps through Europe.

1453 Ottoman Turks capture Constantinople, conquering the Byzantine Empire.

1492 Columbus arrives in North America.

1500s Reformers break away from the Catholic Church, and Protestantism is born.

1776 The U.S. Declaration of Independence is signed.

1789 The French Revolution begins.

1865 The American Civil War ends.

1879 The first practical lightbulb is invented.

SOUTH KOREAN HISTORY

Japan annexes Korea.	**1910**
The March First Movement begins the fight for independence.	**1919**
Korean workers are forced to join the Japanese military.	**1939–1942**
The Korean Peninsula is divided at the 38th parallel.	**1945**
The Republic of Korea is established in the south; the Democratic People's Republic of Korea is established in the north.	**1948**
North Korea invades South Korea, starting the Korean War.	**1950**
The Demilitarized Zone is established as a border between North and South Korea.	**1953**
General Park Chung-hee seizes power in a coup.	**1961**
The army kills hundreds of student demonstrators in Gwangju.	**1979**
Roh Tae-woo wins South Korea's first democratic presidential election.	**1987**
Seoul hosts the Summer Olympic Games.	**1988**
Reunions between North and South Korean relatives are first held.	**2000**
South Korea and Japan cohost the World Cup.	**2002**
South Korea elects its first woman president, Park Geun-hye.	**2012**

WORLD HISTORY

1914	World War I begins.
1917	The Bolshevik Revolution brings communism to Russia.
1929	A worldwide economic depression begins.
1939	World War II begins.
1945	World War II ends.
1969	Humans land on the Moon.
1975	The Vietnam War ends.
1989	The Berlin Wall is torn down as communism crumbles in Eastern Europe.
1991	The Soviet Union breaks into separate states.
2001	Terrorists attack the World Trade Center in New York City and the Pentagon near Washington, D.C.
2004	A tsunami in the Indian Ocean destroys coastlines in Africa, India, and Southeast Asia.
2008	The United States elects its first African American president.

Fast Facts

Official name: Republic of South Korea

Capital: Seoul

Official language: Korean

Seoul

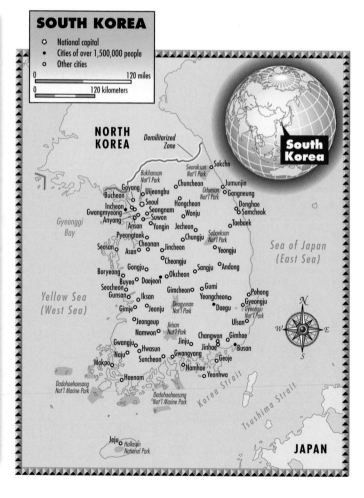

SOUTH KOREA

- ◌ National capital
- • Cities of over 1,500,000 people
- ○ Other cities

0 ——— 120 miles

0 ——— 120 kilometers

NORTH KOREA

Demilitarized Zone

Bukhansan Nat'l Park

Seoraksan Nat'l Park

Sokcho

Goyang Uijeongbu Chuncheon Jumunjin

Bucheon Seoul Odaesan Nat'l Park Gangneung

Incheon Hongcheon Donghae

Gwangmyeong Seongnam Wonju Samcheok

Anyang Suwon

Ansan Yongin Jecheon Taebaek

Gyeonggi Bay

Pyeongtaek Chungju Sobaeksan Nat'l Park

Cheonan Jincheon Sea of Japan (East Sea)

Seosan Asan Yeongju

Cheongju Sangju Andong

Boryeong Gongju Okcheon

Buyeo Daejeon Gumi

Seocheon Gimcheon Yeongcheon Pohang

Gunsan Iksan Gyeongju Nat'l Park

Gimje Jeonju Deogyusan Nat'l Park Daegu Gyeongju

Yellow Sea (West Sea)

Jeongeup Jirisan Nat'l Park Ulsan

Namwon Changwon Gimhae

Gwangju Jinju Jinhae Busan

Hwasun Gwangyang

Naju Suncheon Geoje

Mokpo Namhae

Haenam Yeonhwa

Dadohaehaesang Nat'l Marine Park

Dadohaehaesang Nat'l Marine Park

Korea Strait

Tsushima Strait

Jeju Hallasan National Park

JAPAN

South Korea

National flag

Cheonjiyeon Waterfall

National anthem:	"Aegukka" ("The Patriotic Song")
Government:	Republic
Head of state:	President
Head of government:	President
Area of country:	38,502 square miles (99,720 sq km)
Highest elevation:	Mount Halla, 6,398 feet (1,950 m) above sea level
Lowest elevation:	Sea level along the coast
Length of coastline:	1,499 miles (2,412 km)
Longest river:	Nakdong, 314 miles (505 km)
Largest island:	Jeju, 712 square miles (1,845 sq km)
Average high temperature:	In Seoul, 35°F (2°C) in January, 84°F (29°C) in July
Average low temperature:	In Seoul, 22°F (–6°C) in January, 71°F (22°C) in July
Average annual precipitation:	In Seoul, 57 inches (145 cm)

Dadohaehaesang National Marine Park

Currency

National population (July 2014 est.):	49,039,986	

Population of major cities (2013 est.):

Seoul	10,349,312
Busan	3,678,555
Incheon	2,628,000
Daegu	2,566,540
Daejeon	1,475,221

Landmarks:
- ▶ *Changdeokgung Palace*, Seoul
- ▶ *Dadohaehaesang National Marine Park*, southern and western islands
- ▶ *Manggyeongsa Temple*, Taebaek Mountains
- ▶ *Mount Halla*, Jeju Island
- ▶ *National Museum of Korea*, Seoul

Economy: Most South Koreans work in service industries such as banking, health care, sales, and trade. South Korea has a thriving industrial sector. The country produces electronics, telecommunications equipment, automobiles, chemicals, and steel. Major agricultural crops include rice, cattle, pigs, barley, cabbage, fruit, milk, and eggs. Fishing and aquaculture are important industries in South Korea. The nation's mineral resources include iron, lead, zinc, copper, graphite, and tungsten.

Currency: The South Korea won. In 2014, 1,023 won equaled US$1.

System of weights and measures: Metric system

Literacy rate (2012): 98%

Students

Psy

Common Korean words and phrases:

An-yeong-ha-se-yo.	Hello.
Hwan-yeong-ham-ni-da.	Welcome.
An-yeong-hi ju-mu-sheo-sseo-yo.	Good morning.
Ne. Chal ji-nae-sseo-yo.	I am fine, thanks.
Chal ji-nae-sheo-sseo-yo?	How have you been?
Chom to-wa-ju-shil ssu i-sseu-shi-na-yo?	Could you help me?
I-ge eol-ma-ye-yo?	How much is this?
An-nyeong-hi ga-se-yo.	Good-bye.

Prominent South Koreans:

Ban Ki-moon (1944–)
Secretary general of the United Nations

Bang Jeong-hwan (1899–1931)
Author and founder of Children's Day

Heo Hyeong-man (1947–)
Cartoonist

Park Geun-hye (1952–)
President of South Korea

Inbee Park (1988–)
Golfer

Psy (Park Jae-sang) (1977–)
Singer

Syngman Rhee (1875–1965)
First president of South Korea

Sejong (1397–1450)
King who oversaw a flowering in science and the arts

Yi Sun-sin (1545–1598)
Admiral and inventor of the turtle ship

To Find Out More

Books

▶ Aldridge, Rebecca. *Ban Ki-moon: United Nations Secretary-General*. New York: Chelsea House Publishing, 2009.

▶ Cooper, Alison. *Facts About Buddhism*. New York: Rosen Central, 2010.

▶ Lee, Cecilia Hae-Jin. *Quick and Easy Korean Cooking*. San Francisco: Chronicle Books, 2009.

▶ Perritano, John. *Korean War*. New York: Scholastic, 2010.

Music

▶ Girls' Generation. *The Boys*. Santa Monica, CA: Interscope Records, 2012.

▶ Seoul Music Ensemble. *Korean Traditional Music*. Los Angeles: Zen Arts Publishing, 2010.

▶ Visit this Scholastic Web site for more information on South Korea:
www.factsfornow.scholastic.com
Enter the keywords **South Korea**

Index

Page numbers in *italics*
indicate illustrations.

Meet the Author

BARBARA SOMERVILL HAS been writing children's nonfiction books for more than twenty years. She writes biographies and about countries, earth science, and social studies. Somervill also teaches college writing and critical reading classes. In addition to teaching and writing, she loves movies, theater, baking, and women's softball.

Photo Credits